"You will absolutely love Dr. Edna Ellison's book, *Friendships of Purpose*. With a writing style that is warm, easy to understand, and filled with visual imagery, she unfolds the riches of Paul's letter to the Ephesians. Her ability to make these teachings part of everyday living enables the reader to readily apply them to their personal lives."

—Renee Coates Scheidt
speaker and author, *Bringing Hope to the Heart
Through the Truth of God's Word*

"Like almost every woman I know, my life feels like it is on daily overload. Though the specific stresses and problems change from day to day, I frequently find myself questioning where I will get the energy to make it through another day. What pushes me on? What keeps me going? Knowing that where I am is where God wants me; knowing His purpose for my life and knowing I am fulfilling that. While most women share the stress of an over-full life, few share the success of it: knowing God's purpose. In *Friendships of Purpose*, Edna Ellison combines the reality of an over-full life with the need to know God's will. Perhaps, like me, you cannot carve several hours out of your schedule for weekly Bible study attendance and its accompanying homework, but you can snatch a half hour to catch up with a friend at the coffee shop. Meet with your friend, get a corner table, and connect with God's purpose for your life through *Friendships of Purpose*."

—Marita Littauer
President, CLASServices, Inc.;
speaker and author, *But Lord, I Was Happy Shallow*
and *Your Spiritual Personality*

THE FRIEND TO FRIEND SERIES
BY EDNA ELLISON

*Friend to Friend: Enriching Friendships Through a Shared Study of Philippians*

*Friendships of Faith: A Shared Study of Hebrews*


ALSO BY EDNA ELLISON:

*Woman to Woman: Preparing Yourself to Mentor* (coauthored with Tricia Scribner)

**friend**to**friend**series

# Friendships of Purpose

## A Shared Study of Ephesians

EDNA ELLISON

new
hope
PUBLISHERS
Birmingham, Alabama

New Hope® Publishers
P. O. Box 12065
Birmingham, AL 35202-2065
www.newhopepublishers.com

Library of Congress Cataloging-in-Publication Data

ISBN: 1-56309-901-2

N054106 · 0105 · 6M1

## ▪ ▪ ▪ DEDICATION

To my most precious grands: Blakely Joy Ellison, cherished daughter of Jack and Wendy Ellison, and Eliza Farmer, faithful Boykin Spaniel of Patsy and Tim Farmer. Blakely, may you always remain in God's perfect will, a person of faith and purpose. Eliza, may you remain our family entertainer, our paper-eating, tail-wagging companion.

# ABOUT THE AUTHOR

A popular author and speaker, Edna Ellison has enjoyed leading Bible studies in London, England; Frankfurt, Germany; cities in Panama and Honduras; and in almost every state in America, including Alaska and Hawaii. Her life has been featured in Focus on the Family's *Lifewise*, and her books have been reviewed in *Virtue* and *Publishers Weekly*, among other publications. She has been interviewed on radio and television shows in several states.

Dr. Ellison has an earned Ph.D. from the University of Alabama, an Ed. Spec. degree from the University of South Carolina, an M.A. from Converse College, and a B.A. from Presbyterian College. She has taught at three colleges and two seminaries. She has also served as editor for a national women's magazine and consultant/director of Christian ministries to and by women in several states. She enjoys writing for *Missions Mosaic*, *Christian Single*, and *Missions Leader* magazines, as well as several others. She has written two mentoring books: *Seeking Wisdom* (available from www.ednae9@aol.com) and *Woman to Woman*.

*Friendships of Purpose* is the third in the Friend to Friend series, which are two-by-two Bible studies for friends.

A native of Clinton, South Carolina, Edna Ellison has strong family ties: a son, Jack Martin Ellison, and his wife, Wendy, of Birmingham, Alabama, and their daughter, Blakely; and a daughter, Patsy Ellison Farmer, and her husband, Timothy, of Spartanburg, South Carolina, where Edna Ellison now lives.

# Table of Contents

# ACKNOWLEDGMENTS

This third book in the Friend to Friend series has been an effort of prayer and meditation with every keyboard stroke. It wouldn't have been possible without the encouragement and help of many people.

To Rebecca England, my editor, thank you for your quiet, patient attitude and genuine concern for me as I wrote. Your job was a busy one in the midst of New Hope changes. You have maintained that same steadiness that has endeared you to me through other books you edited in this series. You are indeed a Friend of Purpose!

Andrea Mullins, New Hope's new director, I welcome you as a long-time friend and confidante. You deserve this honor, and I look forward to you sharing your leadership expertise and Christian wisdom with New Hope Publishers. You've shaped my life in joyous ways; thank you for overseeing the birth of this book-baby and ushering it into the world of marketing and promotion.

Thanks also goes to New Hope staff, Tara Miller, Tamzen Benfield, and Kristi Griem for your enthusiastic attention to this project and your expertise in making it a reality!

Thank you, Tricia Scribner, for critiquing this book before it went to the publisher. I appreciate you as a *merea*, professional writer, and Christian friend. I also appreciate Kimberly Sowell, Cherie Nettles, Joy Brown, and Marie Alston—the Women by Design who have stood by me these busy writing days.

I sincerely appreciate my dear friend Fred Crenshaw, who has encouraged my writing, teaching me how to write realistic conversation and describe human nature through the storying process.

To my family: Thank you, Jack, Wendy, and Blakely Ellison, for understanding my busyness and concentration on this book. Thank you, Patsy and Tim Farmer, for sharing your home with me and for demonstrating compassion as I've spent hours glued to the computer in marathon writing sessions.

Most of all, thank You, God, for giving me inspiration when I had none, for filling my mind with words when it was mute, and overflowing my heart with the Spirit when my wellspring was dry. O God, I give this book to You as a labor of love. Thank You for guiding me in my Christian growth, and for birthing this book with joy! "Thanks be to God! He gives us the victory through our Lord Jesus Christ" (1 Corinthians 15:57).

# ■ ■ ■ INTRODUCTION

As you embark on an exciting journey through Ephesians, I pray that God Himself will speak to you though Paul's words. Formerly called Saul of Tarsus, Paul was a well-educated Jewish leader filled with zeal to persecute believers who followed Christ. After his dramatic conversion on the road to Damascus—where he had planned to capture, torture, and kill Christians—Paul began a transformed life as Christianity's best advocate.

The first Christian missionary, he had earlier established a church at Ephesus, and sent a friend, Tychicus, to deliver this epistle, or letter, to the church there to encourage them. Paul wrote this letter from prison in Rome, about A.D. 60. Despite the conditions (probably under house arrest, dependent upon others to provide his food and other items for basic comforts), he wrote with joy and optimism about the future.

If you live in a city, you'll feel a kinship with the Christians in the city of Ephesus, a large commercial metropolis (in present-day Turkey) where two large trade routes crossed. Like many of Paul's letters, this one was written as a "pass-around" letter, sent from church to church, all over Asia Minor.

As you study this book with a friend, a group, or as an individual, I believe you will soon see a strong emerging theme: friendships of purpose. Paul's words about Christ encourage Christians to become like-minded friends, united as the family of God. He urges these brothers and sisters in Christ to focus carefully on a unity of purpose: to serve God and follow *His* will.

May you *focus your life's purpose, define your own mission statement,* and *discern God's eternal design for your life,* as you live it with other Christians in a *united* purpose.

# ▪▪▪ How to Use this Book

If you're picking up this book for the first time, you will find in your hand the answer to these questions:

How do I find God's will for my life?

How do I find self-fulfillment?

How significant am I in the overall scheme of life?

How can I form friendships of purpose?

Where do I fit in the Church?

Where will I go when I die?

Can I actually help God in His plan for the world?

This book is designed to be a **two-by-two Bible study between friends**. Studying Ephesians can enrich your friendships, give you a focused purpose, and draw each of you closer to God. As you share answers from Scriptures and from life, your friendship and your walk with Him will become more spiritually intimate.

Many women use this book (and the others in the Friend to Friend series) as a **group Bible study at church or in homes.** You can study it as a daily devotional five days a week, and then join a group discussion with others once a week for six weeks. Anyone in the group can facilitate the weekly group discussion, sharing the discussion questions in the margins of each chapter.

This book can also be used as an **individual Bible study.** You will enjoy quiet times with the Lord as you explore Paul's words to new Christians in Ephesus. As a new or mature Christian, God speaks through His word as it comes alive in your heart.

You will find the **easy format** a reader-friendly way to approach Scriptural truth. Each of six chapters begins with a poem—which summarizes and mimics Scripture in that chapter—and a short introduction to give you a taste of what's coming in the chapter. Five Bible studies follow, one for each day's devotional/study in that chapter. You will also find suggestions for extra reading as references for deeper study. Each of the thirty studies ends with a Prayer of Purpose, an example for your prayer time.

Are you yearning for spiritual depth and New Testament principles to live by? If you want to live a better life tomorrow than you're living today, *Friendships of Purpose* can give directions for you to find the Way, and to join a friend along the path.

I pray you'll find this an easy-to-understand study to enrich your friendships and your life.

# Unit I

# Lord,

## What's

### My Purpose?

...

GOD IS POSITIVE THAT YOU HAVE A PURPOSE IN LIFE. ARE YOU AS SURE of your purpose? Ephesians will encourage you, pointing to your purpose in the kingdom of God. Good news: you are significant in God's plan! As you study, practical definitions to a few "churchy" words will clarify your purpose.

Look at the next-to-last stanza in the poem below. Part of God's purpose is that you accept His freely-given grace, glory, and forgiveness. Notice the words *wise inheritance*. In God's design for your life, you'll receive wisdom as part of your inheritance. Sound exciting? It is. Ready? Turn the page and begin.

Paul, apostle of Christ Jesus
By the will of God,
Gave good grace and peace to those
Who walked Ephesian sod.

Loved by Jesus and the Father—
Oh, how blessed were they!
Given every spiritual blessing
In a heavenly way.

Jesus, chosen from creation;
Chosen, too, were we.
In His will, adopted sons,
We'll holy, blameless be.

Freely given grace and glory
And forgiveness, too;
Purpose for a wise inheritance—
Heaven and earth in view.

Paul gave thanks for the Ephesians
And for us, who're blessed
To know God's Son raised from the dead,
His Name above the rest.

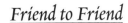

## Study I

# *I'm Finding My Purpose*

EPHESIANS 1:1–3

ON THE WAY HOME FROM SHOPPING, FIVE-YEAR-OLD RUSTY Martin, my nephew, sat in the back seat of my car, talking about "Wheel." After a few moments I realized he was talking about his friend Will Ferguson, whose name he pronounced "Wheel."

Years later, Will Ferguson grew up and worked at our local bank. He really was a "wheel." I got a loan because he knew me personally. I laughed with Will as we recalled the days when Rusty called him "Wheel."

Will and I understood each other. He knew he could trust me, and I knew I could trust him. Our agreement didn't have anything to do with the bank's management or its reputation. It was a matter of personal character, a bond between Will and me. In our small town, I had known his father and mother for years. My husband trusted that family; we would have done anything for them. According to Webster, will can mean "power to control by mental force"; "determination"; or "a testament." As a verb, "to determine; to bequeath, as to will a fortune to an heir; or to express probability or inevitability" in the future, as "I will . . ."

In today's study we'll look at several facets of God's will. Paul begins his advice to the church members in Ephesus by talking about how the will of God relates to him and to them.

*Friend to Friend*

What does "finding God's will" mean to you?

Share your answers with a friend.

## Last Will and Testament

From the New Testament passage below (Ephesians 1:1–3), circle words and/or phrases that have significant meaning to you:

"Paul, an apostle of Christ Jesus by the will of God, to the saints in Ephesus, the faithful in Christ Jesus: Grace and peace to you from God our Father and the Lord Jesus Christ. Praise be to the God and Father of our Lord Jesus Christ, who has blessed us in the heavenly realms with every spiritual blessing in Christ."

Which words did you circle? I circled *apostle, Christ Jesus, will of God, saints, faithful, Christ Jesus, praise, God and Father, our Lord, Jesus Christ, blessed us, heavenly realms, spiritual blessing,* and *Christ.*

Write below the reasons you circled the words you chose from Ephesians 1:1–3:

Did you find any words repeated? List them below:

As I read the passage above, I saw one word-pair used four times: Christ Jesus, Christ Jesus, Jesus Christ, and Jesus Christ. Christ is the Greek translation of the Hebrew Messiah, used in the Old Testament to point Jewish people to the One who would come to save His people from their sins. In the New Testament, above anything else, Paul points to Jesus as Messiah!

How does Paul identify himself?

How does He identify church members?

Besides identifying Jesus as the Christ, or Messiah, Paul also identifies himself as an apostle, one sent, writing to the saints in the church at Ephesus. In a greater sense, God speaks through these words to us as today's saints, ones faithful in Christ Jesus. **If you're a Christian, you can count yourself as one of the faithful, therefore, a saint. How can Paul be designated as an apostle and you as a saint?** You may not feel very saintly, but notice that Paul says he's an apostle because of the will of God, who also has the power to designate you as a faithful saint.

Can you become saintly by using your will power to be perfect? Can you become a saint by your determination, or iron will, to be good? As we study Paul's letter to the Ephesian saints, we will explore how you and I attain sainthood, even if we know we have not lived perfect, godly lives. *Extra reading:* You'll find a clue in Ephesians 3:8–9.

## I Am Weak and He Is Strong. . .

Paul ends the third verse with a song of praise to the God of Purpose, the source of all our goodness. Look at it again: "Praise be to the God and Father of our Lord Jesus Christ, who has blessed us in the heavenly realms with *every spiritual blessing* in Christ." God has purpose for His will: His will is to bless you. He wants to give you many spiritual blessings from heavenly realms!

Now compare the last sentence above to verse 3. How many spiritual blessings does God want to give you? He does

What does *apostle* mean?

What does *saint* mean?

In your opinion, how does one become saintly?

not say "many," but _____ spiritual blessings. What do you think that means? When your will matches God's will, when you welcome a personal relationship with Him, He is able to reconcile both your will and His will; and, through Christ, you can find your purpose in life.

**Circle** descriptions of **your** mind/will, then **underline** descriptions of **God's** mind/will:

infinite, can't touch
finite, concrete
ultimate
simple
incomprehensible
wishy-washy
heavenly
earthly
super-smart
duh
low
high

How do you feel about coordinating your will and purpose with that of Almighty God?

Religious experts suggest a variety of ways you can mesh your will with God's will. I have one simple suggestion: start with praise. Verses 1–3 form a song of praise. Begin praising Him by meditating on these three verses. Then pray the Prayer of Purpose.

## A Prayer of Purpose

*Lord, I praise You for the apostle Paul, who learned the secret of making Your will his own. Help me do as He did.* **Show me clearly Your will for my life.** *Teach me to be faithful, like the saints in Ephesus, embracing Your purpose for my life. Amen.*

# Study 2

# I'm Adopted into God's Family

EPHESIANS 1:4–6

ONE NIGHT I HAD A DREAM ABOUT CREATION. GOD WAS BUSY dividing the earth from the waters. Mighty billows of water were in upheaval; dirt and sand swirled around, finally settling together to form continents. The movement was massive. Just as God was about to hurl great boulders together, He paused, as if thinking to Himself, and said, "Oh, yes—I want Edna to be holy."

Write your first name in the blanks below:

God wants _____ to be holy.

God is holy; His children were born to be holy, in the image of God.

God is holy; I, _____, His child, was born to be holy.

Is this an unrealistic dream? If you think so, read Ephesians 1:4–6. Isn't it incredible that even before the creation of the world, God chose you to be holy and blameless? Do you

Can you believe God chose you to be holy and blameless before He created the world? Why or why not?

remember when you first heard this concept? What do you think about it?

A pastor once said to my husband after a worship service, "Sons *inherit* His will and *inherit in* His will." We went home and talked about this new concept: Since God chose us, adopted us into His family, we're His children; we belong to Him. Born-again children in the "Christian" clan are heirs of all God owns. "If you belong to Christ, then you are . . . heirs according to the promise" (Galatians 3:29). Our Father promises you can inherit "every blessing" (Study 1) and become an heir in His will (His written last will and testament, the New Testament)!

## My Father's House

When you're adopted, you're invited to live in God's home forever—but first, He makes His home in you. The Bible describes God's house in many ways. Here are four foundational pillars of faith confirming your reservation in the Home of all Homes:

**Pillar 1: Predestination**— Paul says, "He predestined us to be adopted . . . in accordance with his pleasure and will" (Ephesians 1:5). God wills for us to be adopted, that is, to accept Jesus Christ as our Savior and become members of the family of God. There's unlimited room in our Father's house; His purpose is that everyone—"whoever believes" (John 3:16)—is accepted as His child, heir to His promises. (Read more about predestination in Study 4.) *Extra reading:* Matthew 24:22, 31; Acts 4:28; Romans 8:29, 33; 2 Timothy 2:10, James 2:5; 1 Peter 1:2, 20.

**Pillar 2: Propitiation**— Primitive peoples used a propitiation to please ancient gods, to appease their wrath and prevent punishment. Paul uses the words, "in love . . . through Jesus Christ" (Ephesians 1:4–5). How did your Heavenly Father, in accordance with His pleasure and will, arrange for you to become a member of the family? By sending your Brother, Jesus, as a *sacrifice, atonement,* or *propitiation* for your sins. *Extra reading:* Romans 3:25, 1 John 2:2, 4:10

**Pillar 3: Salvation**— Paul says, "to the praise of his glorious grace, which he has freely given us in the One he loves" (Ephesians 1:6). The One whom God loves is Jesus. God Himself sacrificed His only Son to provide salvation, or save you from punishment in hell, where the goodness and joy of your Father are absent. He gave salvation freely—at no cost to you, but great cost to Him—according to His grace. In one fell swoop, you received adoption and salvation!

**Pillar 4: Sanctification**— Paul says we're chosen "to be holy and blameless in his sight" (Ephesians 1:4). After predestination by the Father's will, propitiation through the Son, and salvation given by His glorious grace, God makes you holy. Notice who sees you as perfect: God! When you enter heaven, instead of proclaiming your good works (for example: "I taught Sunday School and went on a mission trip"), you just say, "I believe Jesus died for me, as my propitiation (atonement). He redeemed me—**on purpose!**" Then, as a member of the family of God, you enter, claiming His promise of eternal life!

### Friend to Friend

In your own words, describe the four pillars of faith.

My Father's House

Predestination   Propitiation   Salvation   Sanctification

And here's a special promise: God is working in you now. In your relationship with your heavenly Father, you begin to learn from Him daily, aligning your will with His, refining your heart, and becoming more holy-and-blameless in His sight. Your actions will progressively reflect a purer heart as slowly you reject the carnal side of yourself and walk in the light of His Spirit.

If you have questions about the words you've studied, ask your pastor or study friend about them.

## Chumming Up Churchy Words

We've "chummed up" four churchy words by taking a closer look. I hope you're feeling more comfortable with the family dialect. Paul wrote this letter to the new converts in Ephesus, who desperately needed his explanation of these pillars of Christianity. We'll shed more light on these details in the next few studies.

## A Prayer of Purpose

*Thank You, Lord, for salvation so simple a child can understand. You accepted me just as I am and loved me enough to die for me, according to Your will and purpose. Continue to work in me, making me sanctified—holy and blameless in Your sight. Amen.*

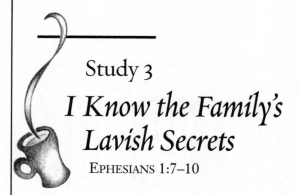

## Study 3

# I Know the Family's Lavish Secrets

EPHESIANS 1:7–10

UNCLE BOB, GOVERNOR OF SOUTH CAROLINA, WAS MY favorite uncle. Our family was proud of him and visited him often. As a schoolgirl, I bragged about how wonderful and famous he was. Then in our high school library I found a book about governors. I couldn't wait to see what it said about Uncle Bob. When I looked up his name, I found: "Only South Carolina governor to be impeached in office." I was mortified. I never dragged any family skeletons out of the closet again!

Most of us have something we don't tell about our families. In the human family, shame is everywhere: in your immediate family, the extended family, your work group, school classrooms, or neighborhood gatherings.

Were you ever embarrassed about a skeleton in your family's closet? Explain, if you feel comfortable sharing.

Pray now for a person you know who is often ashamed. Ask God what you can do to affirm that person and help diminish some of her/his shame.

However, the secrets in the family of God are not shameful or scandalous; they are lavish "nest eggs," treasures for the future. Paul says, "In him we have redemption through his blood, the forgiveness of sins, in accordance with the riches of God's grace that he lavished on us with all wisdom and understanding. And he made known to us the mystery of his will according to his good pleasure, which he purposed in Christ, to be put into effect when the times will have reached their fulfillment—to bring all things in heaven and on earth together under one head, even Christ" (Ephesians 1:7–10).

*Friend to Friend*

## What's the Big Mystery?

The *mystery of God's will* was that Jesus would become a sacrifice for you. What is your definition of sacrifice? Write it in the margin.

A sacrifice is a sacrifice only if the thing sacrificed, or given up, is cherished. God offered His best, His only Son, who experienced temptation as a human, but never sinned. His heart was pure and His deeds were perfectly motivated. God gave His best, unblemished Lamb to be sacrificed for you. (Read more about redemption through the blood of the Lamb in Study 8.)

A few years ago, our church had a food drive. A woman who called me said, "Just bring a few cans of beets. I hate beets! I'm always glad to get rid of any in my pantry!" I'm sure she thought she had made a worthy contribution, a sacrifice for the hungry people in our community. A home-cooked turkey dinner, with all the trimmings, delivered to a hungry family after five hours of labor in the kitchen may have been a worthier sacrifice. What do you think?

If you give extravagantly, but the gift costs you little, it's not a sacrifice; it's like a sounding brass gong or a tinkling cymbal, a sound in the wind, quickly fading (1 Corinthians 13:1–3). Your "sacrifice" may lack worth, meaning, or purpose; but here's the best part of God's love: He has **purpose**—solid intentions for you in His sacrifice. He says, "My purpose is that they may be encouraged in heart and united in love, so that they may have *the full riches of complete understanding*, in order that they may know the mystery of God, namely, Christ, in whom are hidden all the treasures of wisdom and knowledge" (Colossians 2:2–3).

## What Was God's Purpose?

Did Christ know what He was doing? According to Paul, He lavished His riches upon us with all wisdom and understanding (Ephesians 1:8). He willingly—knowing full well the torture, pain, and death—went to the cross for you.

He intended His sacrifice to be a free gift: "I will *give* you the . . . riches stored in secret places" (Isaiah 45:3). Good news!

This is a family secret you can tell everyone! "If you call out for insight and cry aloud for understanding, and if you look for it as for silver and search for it as for hidden treasure, then you will understand the fear of the Lord and find the knowledge of God" (Proverbs 2:3–5). You can share—or make known "the mystery of His will . . . which he purposed in Christ" (Ephesians 1:9)—with people who don't have a clue about how to find God.

What do you think God's purpose may be for your life?

What ideas does Paul give you in Ephesians 1 that you may use to find and explore your purpose in life?

Share your ideas with your study partner.

Before you read the Prayer of Purpose for today, read Jeremiah 33:3, asking God to show you His purpose during this Bible study of Ephesians.

Paul says in Ephesians 1:10 that when the time is ready to be fulfilled, Christ will be the head of all things in heaven and on earth. How is He the head over your heart now? Do you bow before Him out of a grateful heart? Pray that you will be submissive to His will, allowing Him to be your sovereign Lord. Pray that you will find the lavish family secrets through Bible study and prayer, and that you will seek His will as you decide what to do with the riches of God's mysteries.

*Friend to Friend*

## A Prayer of Purpose

*Awesome Lord, owner of all riches, thank You for giving me salvation through Christ's sacrifice. Help me handle family secrets without shame.* **I seek peace with the past, the mysteries of Your wisdom for today, and Your will and purpose for the future.** *Amen.*

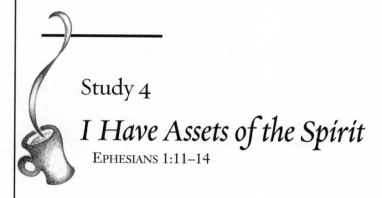

## Study 4

# I Have Assets of the Spirit

EPHESIANS 1:11–14

AFTER MY HUSBAND DIED, MY DAUGHTER PATSY AND I WENT to her college orientation, including a financial aid meeting. The aid officer figured that without my husband's salary to count on to pay for tuition, Patsy would qualify. Humm. Too bad—my husband's life insurance gave us assets, so we had borrowing power for college loans. There'd be no government grants for us.

Then he explained another option: if a family had more than one student in school at a time, the college placed it in another category. If I went back to school, grants would provide Patsy's room, board, tuition, and books! I hesitated a few seconds and then signed. For four years I earned Patsy's schooling by going to school myself. God had plans we'd never known: "'I know the plans I have for you,' declares the Lord, "plans to prosper you and not to harm you, plans to give you hope and a future" (Jeremiah 29:11).

## His Master Plan

Read the plan God has for you in Ephesians 1:11–14. Delving into these verses, look for words connected to *Him* or *His* that show the characteristics of His plan for you. Then fill in the following with *Him* or *His*:

I'm chosen in _____, according to the plan of _____ who works out everything with the purpose of _____ will. I have hope in _____, for the praise of _____ glory. I was included in _____, when I heard the word of truth, the gospel of my salvation.

List four risks you'd have to take in order to conform to God's will.

1.

2.

3.

4.

List four reasons why you'd want to conform to God's will.

1.

2.

3.

4.

### Friend to Friend

Does Edna's story of the surprise financial aid remind you of a time God blessed you with a gift? What happened?

Share your answers with your study friend.

## Four Spiritual Assets

### 1. CHOSEN IN HIM

*Predestination:* Remember in Study 2 when we looked at this word? Write in your own words what it means:

God will never violate you or deny your free will. However, His ideal plan is that you hope in Christ, *for the purpose of His will,* to the praise of His glory. When you say "yes" to God's salvation plan, accepting Christ into your heart, *His* plan becomes *your* asset. When the earth is shaking all around you, when you can't depend on others—when your world makes no sense—you can hold on to hope in Christ, finding comfort in being predestined according to God's plan.

One way to look at predestination is experiential: you start your journey up a mountain toward God. While making progress uphill, occasionally you fall off a hairpin curve, wandering until you find the high road again. Finally at the top, you look back. The road looks straighter in retrospect. God says, "I knew you'd make it; that was My plan." While experiencing the journey of life, you weren't aware of God's protective hand, but looking back, you realize you couldn't have made it without Him. You don't take credit for your godly progress along the way; you praise Him for His help and guidance.

### 2. CONFORMING TO THE PURPOSE OF HIS WILL

*Conformity:* Though postmodern Americans don't generally admire conformity (to "peer pressure" or "the company line"), conformity in any situation offers safety. No safety is as dependable as that of conformity to the purpose of His will. Notice why we obediently conform (Ephesians 1:11–12): to align our wills with the **purpose** of God's will, hoping in Christ for the praise of His glory.

### 3. Believing the Gospel of Salvation

*Salvation:* This is the ultimate asset: it guarantees everlasting life. What a wonderful miracle God gives us! As Paul says, "You also were included in Christ when you heard the word of truth, the gospel of your salvation" (Ephesians 1:13). Your Redeemer's sacrifice redeems—"cashes in"—your ticket into heaven, where you find eternal salvation from harm.

Read verse 13 again, as Paul explains, "the word of truth, the gospel [good news] of salvation." Reading your Bible and listening to gospel preaching are key activities to your understanding spiritual truth.

### 4. Marked with the Spirit's Seal

*Seal of the Holy Spirit:* God promises (in verse 14) the Holy Spirit as a deposit guaranteeing your inheritance until you're redeemed, meeting God face to face. God's Spirit comes as your Advocate, Counselor, and Comforter—a Presence that assures you God is real.

God's Word says, "I will make you like my signet ring, for I have chosen you" (Haggai 2:23). A signet ring stamped into wax becomes a seal, a solemn vow. God has chosen you, and His seal guarantees your future.

Think of other spiritual assets God has for us. List them here:

*Friend to Friend*

Share your reason for listing each asset.

*A Prayer of Purpose*

*Lord, thank You for choosing me, providing my plan. Help me conform to Your will. I place my hope in You, living for the praise of Your glory.* **I submit to Your will now;** *mark me as Your daughter; seal me as Yours until I see You face to face in heaven. Amen.*

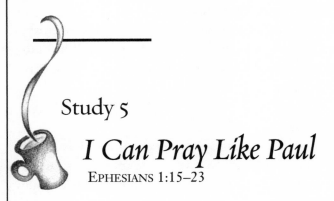

## Study 5

# I Can Pray Like Paul

EPHESIANS 1:15–23

Are your prayers simply copies of what you've heard in your church?

List favorite phrases you've heard in the prayers of God's people.

IN 1993 I MOVED TO FRESNO, CALIFORNIA, AND FOUND several astounding things: a church on every corner, not many "fruits, nuts, and flakes" (as I'd heard), and the abundant prayers of God's people! Every area has a different culture, but I experienced reverse culture shock I hadn't expected: the fervent prayers of fervent saints.

In a church I visited, a man kneeling at the altar prayed, "Lord, I come to You in the most humble way I know how. We're painfully aware we could never make ourselves humble enough before You to be blameless in Your sight. We are not worthy to eat the crumbs beneath Your table, but Lord, we beg You for mercy." Tears flowed—in my eyes as well as his—as he continued to pray with Christlike humility. That prayer changed my life. The pray-er enriched my prayer life.

Most Christians learn to pray from hearing the prayers of other Christians. How about you? Do you recall how you learned to pray? Let's read about Paul's prayers in Ephesians 1:15–19a.

## Praying Prayers of Purpose

In this letter to new Christians in Ephesus, Paul outlines his prayers for them **as they form friendships of purpose**. His prayers aren't wishy-washy and weak; they show a solid purpose of intercession. Remember the last pillar, or basic principle, of Christianity in Study 2? Notice how Paul prays that the Ephesians grow in their fullness of Christ, or their *saintliness*. He prays for their *sanctification*, as they grow more Christ-centered, less Me-centered.

He says, "ever since I heard about . . ." (—two things. Name them below.)

What two things did Paul hear about the new Christians in Ephesus?

1.

2.

Tell your study friend how she demonstrates these qualities.

Why is the order of these two things important? First, Paul gives thanks for the Ephesians' salvation, and then he prays for them to know Christ better, so they can love the saints better. In other words, he's praying for their sanctification, that they'll be so filled with Christ that their love will overflow and cover other saints. You can love the saints completely only after, in faith, you've asked Christ to be Lord of your heart.

Following Paul's model prayer outline (Ephesians 1:15–19a), write down words from the Scripture passage that show the following ways to pray:

• Give thanks for members of your church family.

## Friend to Friend

Write a humble prayer now, sincerely talking to God:

Do you know a saint (a Christian) who's hard to love? Someone at church? In the family?

Share your frustrations with your study friend.

• Intercede for others in the Christian family.
　　a) Ask continually for the Spirit of wisdom for them.
　　b) Seek spiritual revelation, for them to know Him better.
　　c) Pray that their eyes will be enlightened.
• Know (accept into your heart as you pray) the hope to which He calls you.
• Know (accept as a fact) the riches of glorious inheritance in the saints (you).
• Know (accept and use) His great power.

Write down the words you selected from Ephesians 1:15–19:

## Pumping Iron: Examine the Power

The next few verses explain God's power; read Ephesians 1:19b–23 now.

　　Paul paints a picture through strong language: *"power . . . working . . . mighty strength . . . exerted."* What a vigorous, mighty God! But Paul continues describing what happened after God exerted His strength by raising Christ from the dead; He seated Christ at His right hand (in a position of power like the seated position of a ruler/rabbi as he taught in the temple),

　　Above all rule,
　　Above all authority,
　　Above all power and dominion,
　　Above all titles,
　　Above all time.

A western ranch owner once said, "Take a look at the back forty. It's family territory: long and high and deep and wide!" Praise your Father for what you'll inherit in heaven!

## A Prayer of Purpose

*Lord, fill me with Your love so I can love others, especially* _____ *in my church and* _____ *in my family. Your power is awesome, Almighty God.* **Fill my heart with Your power and purpose,** *in the name of Jesus, high and lifted up. Amen.*

## Friend to Friend

# Unit 2

# *Lord,*

### *Introduce Me to My Family*

■ ■ ■

GET READY! EPHESIANS 2 WILL GIVE YOU AN OVERVIEW OF your progress in the faith: first dead in sin, then saved because He loves you even in your sin. From His overflowing peace and grace, He gave you new life in Christ, to hope in Him, approach His throne with confidence, love all people, and change from *stranger* into *citizen* of heaven.

**God has a purpose for you, but you won't fulfill it alone.** He surrounds you with a support group: the family of God. Want to hear more about it? Turn the page and begin!

Sons of disobedience walking
With the prince of air;
Though we're dead in our transgressions,
Jesus shows His care.

You've been saved by grace, through faith
(Not us, but Holy Ghost);
It's a gift, not done by works,
Lest anyone should boast.

You are God's own workmanship . . .
(Do the things He's planned!)
Separated once from God,
Now brought near His hand.

Don't walk in the flesh and sin, but
Now walk through the wall,
Joining Gentiles and the Jews,
His cross brings peace to all.

Reconciling far and near . . .
Strangers become one.
Foundation of the house of God,
Jesus, Cornerstone!

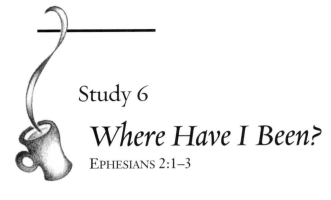

Study 6

# Where Have I Been?

EPHESIANS 2:1–3

WHEN JACK WAS FIVE, I BOUGHT NEW AREA RUGS AT WHOLE-sale prices. Proud of my bargains, for which I had saved a long time, I laid the lush green rugs in my living room and dining room with a grand-opening unveiling! In the next few days, Jack adored the fluffy pile and spent many hours playing with his miniature cars in the "jungle" of green yarn. One day he "decorated" the rugs with a red indelible marker, to make a few roads!

With no hope of salvaging the rugs, I sadly threw them in the trash—but not before I gave a tongue lashing to my "son of disobedience." I'll never forget his puzzled look as he explained he was trying to make the rugs look better!

Have you ever fallen into disobedience and not recognized it? Like my son, you've probably been surprised that your own behavior was wrong. You've regretted something you did on purpose or accidentally, but it was too late to take back what you'd done.

Identify several things you've done almost without thinking, or in ignorance, later regretting them.

What were your feelings after you realized the seriousness of what you did?

What did you learn from these experiences?

## Dead from the Neck Up

Have you ever felt dead from the neck up? If you're like most people, occasionally you don't think before you act. You may have felt numb to the Holy Spirit's influence on your life. See how Paul describes this condition: "As for you, you were dead in your transgressions and sins, in which you used to live when you followed the ways of this world and of the ruler of the kingdom of the air, the spirit who is now at work in those who are disobedient. All of us also lived among them at one time, gratifying the cravings of our sinful nature and following its desires and thoughts. Like the rest, we were by nature objects of wrath" (Ephesians 2:1–3).

Paul speaks to "you." Who is "you"? What words in the next sentence signify that "you" is plural? Paul is correct: *all of us* have lived "dead" lives at times. How can you be alive and dead at the same time? Paul's Greek word for *dead* in verse 1 is *yathar*, or *remnant*, perhaps of a plant, hacked to the ground, barely living—like us, at times, *living* to "follow the ways of this world" and its possessions—and yet "*dead* in our transgressions and sins." Proverbs 11:28 explains, "A life devoted to things is a dead life, a stump; a God-shaped life is a flourishing tree" (*The Message*).

Do you go through periods feeling you're "really living it up," only to discover you're really brain dead (like a stump)—not thinking logically or living with any *purpose*?

## Dead Through Our Nature

Just as Adam and Eve committed the first sin in the Garden of Eden, all of us have sinned. Eve sinned out of ignorance, first listening to Satan, and then falling for his lies. Then Adam, *knowing* God's rules and *considering good*, chose *evil* when Eve offered it. Because both of them sinned willingly, our God of justice had to enforce justice and punish them. We are, by nature, part of fallen creation, inheritors of the legacy of Adam and Eve's sin. All have sinned—even Paul, the apostle! "All have sinned and fall short of the glory of God" (Romans 3:23).

Give your definition of the following phrases in Ephesians 2:1–3:

• dead in your transgressions and sins


• the ways of this world


• the ruler of the kingdom of the air


• the spirit who is now at work in those who are disobedient


• gratifying the cravings of our sinful nature


• following its desires and thoughts


• by nature objects of wrath


Since the Fall of Adam and Eve, we are by nature sinful, hiding our sin from the wrath of our parents, our pastors, and even

God. You and I might as well admit it: we are sinners! (Everyone is.) When you hide sin, you deny it ever existed. You bury it inside, putting off the inevitable: facing that you're a sinner who's followed the ways of the world (Satan's kingdom). When you refuse to admit you've flirted with the "ruler of the kingdom of the air," you block spiritual healing through confession and commitment to a relationship with Christ.

Circle actions you consider "ways of the world":

• Watching unwholesome things on television or the computer
• Thinking of going to bed with an attractive person of the opposite sex
• Deciding not to tell a friend something you did to her, to keep from hurting her feelings
• Taking a few paper clips and pens from work
• Getting extra help off someone's paper at school, during an exam
• Letting a profane word slip out of your mouth—but you were provoked
• Hoping an acquaintance won't come to your church and interfere with your relationships there
• Spending your tithe on a new car

Of the examples of lust, lies, stealing, swearing, jealousy, and greed, which did you identify as worldly ways? Most people can identify with more than one.

In the Garden of Eden, God called to Adam and Eve: "Where are you?" (Genesis 3:9). God knew where they were, but He sought relationship with them even as they hid from Him in their sin. Because of His great love for us, He still calls us out of sin into relationship with Him. As you pray today, consider these questions: Where have you been? Where are you now?

## A Prayer of Purpose

*Lord, forgive me for sins I've committed. As a sinner, I don't deserve Your mercy, but I'm grateful for it. Help me remember my past, confess sins there, and depend on Your power, far greater than Satan's power, to* **keep me clean and pure here and now.** *Amen.*

Study 7

# From Death to Life

EPHESIANS 2:4–7

LOIS ROBINETTE, A FRIEND FROM ENNIS, TEXAS, ASKED ME TO speak at a city-wide banquet. The scriptural theme, decided months before the event, was "But I, when I am lifted up from the earth, will draw all men to myself" (John 12:32). She and I sat at the back of a giant room with hundreds of women. A soft-spoken young woman came to the podium and said, "Welcome to our banquet. I hope you will enjoy our time together."

*Pretty weak welcome*, I thought.

Another young woman stepped up to the stage, blew into the microphone, and said, "Let us pray. Thank You, Lord, for the food. Amen."

*Weak prayer, too*, I said to myself.

A third young woman made a few announcements, and the banquet began.

After we ate, I spoke about keys for living Christian lives: we must take humble positions and lift Jesus high before us. (I admit I was proud of what I said, and rightly so, because I had studied the Scriptures, planned the right words, and practiced for weeks! It was a "hula-hoop moment"—my head was so big that it required a hula-hoop for a headband.)

On the way home I asked, "Lois, why didn't *you* welcome everyone? You're a dynamic speaker. You could've done a much better job than the woman who gave the welcome. She looked twelve years old. When *you* pray, the windows of heaven open! And announcements would've been clear if a confident woman like you had given them."

Lois replied, "Edna, when the spotlight comes up, mature Christian women need to be in the background. I'm mentoring those young women. I want *them* in the limelight, not me. I'm like their agent. This is the first time they've been on stage; they came alive tonight! Maybe you thought they seemed hesitant, but they won't be next time! They'll be stars, shining Jesus' love to others. As their 'star agent,' I am proud of them!" (For more about being a star agent, read *Woman to Woman: Preparing Yourself to Mentor*, available from New Hope Publishers.)

I said no more. I was ashamed of myself that night. Hypocrite and sinner, I had not practiced what I preached. I had proclaimed humility yet had not demonstrated it. I had been critical and "dead in transgressions." I hadn't even recognized wonderful mentoring and the riches of God's grace Lois was giving those young women.

Do you recall a time when you didn't recognize God's grace and riches?

## God Makes Us Alive

Study 6 asked you to concentrate on your sin—your spiritual deadness—and your need for God. Read Ephesians 2:4–7 to see what God says about coming back from spiritual death to spiritual life. Let's dissect this passage:

**God,**
[Describe Him.] **who is rich in mercy,**
[Did what?] **made us alive with Christ,**
[Why?] **because of his great love,**

I remember when I first stood to say something before a crowd. Here's what happened:

Share with your study friend. Then read the "dissect this passage" section as a responsive reading.

[For whom?] **for us,**
[When?] **even when we were dead,**
[Dead? Really? How were we dead?] **dead in transgressions—things we'd done to God and others.**
[How did He do that?] **by grace you've been saved.**
[That's unbelievable! What else did God do?] **Two things: He**
    **1) raised us up with Christ and**
    **2) seated us with Him**
[Where?] **in heavenly realms.**
[That's unbelievable! In heaven?] **Yes,**
[How?] **in Christ Jesus,**
[Why?] **in order that He might show the incomparable riches,**
[Which riches?] **riches of His grace.**
[When?] **in the coming ages—like the 21st century.**
[How's that expressed?] **in His kindness.**
[Whose kindness?] **God's kindness,**
[Expressed *in whom*?] **in Jesus Christ,**
[Expressed *to whom*?] **to us.**
[That's unbelievable!] **No, that's just my point. It's believable if you believe.**

You can believe this incredible promise. You *will* be sitting next to Christ, who sits in a position of power in the heavenly realms!

## From Death to Life: Come Alive!

How about it? Right now, will you do something on purpose? Will you come alive, in a greater way than ever before, believing in Him on purpose? Spread your branches, like Lois, growing as a "star agent," passing along the seeds of vigorous life as you lift up Jesus before others. Form friendships of purpose, one by one, with those who are growing alongside you and behind you. Accept the riches of His grace first; then, *purpose in your heart* to pass along those riches to another person. Change from a dead stump to a seed-bearing tree!

*A Prayer of Purpose*

Lord, **give me the purpose of looking for Your unbelievable grace** in my life every day. Thank You for giving me salvation through Jesus Christ, raising me up, and seating me with Christ in heaven. O, Lord, I believe! And I'll share the riches with friends. Amen.

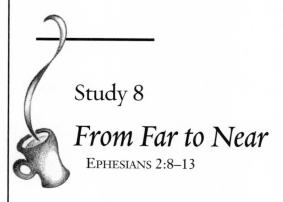

## Study 8

# *From Far to Near*

EPHESIANS 2:8–13

ANYTIME ONE MEETS A FORMER U.S. FIRST LADY, regardless of politics, it is a special occasion. In 1986 a magazine assigned me to interview Rosalyn Carter in Atlanta. I met her at a hotel and wrote a cover story about her volunteer work with Habitat for Humanity, her struggle with parenting while living in the White House, and her sympathy for foreign leaders' widows, who became her personal friends. I'll always remember one thing she said: Wherever Americans go, people know about it. Every shepherd on every Andes hill gets instant news through modern media like transistor radios (wireless laptops today). People in remote areas are not excluded from any happening.

We're also not excluded *spiritually*, even if we live in remote *spiritual places*, far away from God. We have **access to His omnipresent grace**: "For it is by grace you have been saved, through faith—and this not from yourselves, it is the gift of God—not by works, so that no one can boast. For we are

God's workmanship, created in Christ Jesus to do good works, which God prepared in advance for us to do. Therefore, remember that formerly you who are Gentiles by birth and called 'uncircumcised' by those who call themselves 'the circumcision' (that done in the body by the hands of men)— remember that at that time you were separate from Christ, excluded from citizenship in Israel and foreigners to the covenants of the promise, without hope and without God in the world. But now in Christ Jesus you who once were far away have been brought near through the blood of Christ" (Ephesians 2:8–13).

## You're a Piece of Work

You are the handiwork of Almighty God! He created you as a unique, gifted individual, unlike anyone else on earth, designed to have a purpose in His kingdom's work among His Church (extra reading: Psalm 139). Here are six things to learn from today's Scripture passage:

1. Grace is God's gift to you.
2. You don't work to become saved from your sins, but . . .
3. God prepared in advance the work you're to do.
4. You were once separated, excluded, and foreign to the covenants of God's promise.
5. Without God, you're without hope.
6. The blood of Jesus brings you from *far* away to *near* God.

For the 6 points on this page, write what you think each one means:

1.


2.

3.

4.

5.

6.

Future Ephesians studies will explore some of these principles. Today's study concentrates on number 6: Jesus' blood brings us near God.

God says *blood represents life* (Leviticus 17:11). In Old Testament days believers showed God they loved Him with a blood sacrifice, which represented their giving Him life itself. As years passed, the faithful bought live animals, usually unblemished lambs, goats, or heifers, for sacrifices. (They *bought redemption* for sins.) Paul explained, "In him we have redemption through his blood, the forgiveness of sins" (Ephesians 1:7). Jesus, the Lamb of God, redeemed us, buying us with His blood—He sacrificed His very lifeblood for you!

The Bible speaks often about being cleansed by the blood of the Lamb. As a child, I never understood how blood cleansed. It seemed dirty, messy to me. God has now shown me a beautiful truth: the ingredients of animal sacrifice are the ingredients of soap, which cleanses.

## The Perfect Cleanser

My grandmother made lye soap in a washpot, using three main ingredients. First she heated "animal renderings" (lard or tallow) and water. She added lye (acid), a catalyst, which combined with water to change the ingredients into soap as they cooled.

Imagine Old Testament women, washing clothes on river rocks downstream from the tabernacle, who noticed the residue from the tabernacle-sacrifices caused a miracle. Suds began to form; their clothes seemed cleaner, purer. The blood, combined with other elements of sacrifice, became a cleansing agent! Hebrews 9:13–14 says, "The blood of goats and . . . ashes [chemically, an acid] of a heifer sprinkled on those who are ceremonially unclean sanctify them so that they are outwardly clean. How much more, then, will the blood of Christ . . .cleanse our consciences from acts that lead to death, so that we may serve the living God!"

This chart represents the miracle of blood-cleansing:

| Time: | Old Testament | New Testament | Grandmother's day |
|---|---|---|---|
| Cleanser: | Lamb | Jesus | Soap |
| Oil Ingredient: | Animal Blood | Divine/Human Blood | Tallow/lard |
| Acid: | Ashes | Vinegar (on hyssop) | Lye |
| Liquid: | River Water | Sweat, tears | Water/heat |
| Reaction: | Suds | Miracle of Holy Spirit | Chemical reaction |
| Results: | Clean Rocks, etc. | Resurrection and Salvation | Cleanser for clothes |

What a mystery! At the cross, all the elements of cleansing were represented. The oil element: the blood of Christ; the acid element: vinegar given to Our Lord on hyssop; and the water element: sweat and tears of His suffering. The reaction, caused by a supernatural miracle of God's Holy Spirit, resulted in resurrection and salvation—perfect cleansing for you and me!

What do you think of Edna's theory of cleansing?

Has God cleansed you, giving you new life? Explain.

This is the gospel, the good news! Paul says **we have access to it**. In your world today, how accessible is the daily news? Do you have access to the good news of Jesus? If you're in the family of God, He draws you near to hear it! Hallelujah!

## A Prayer of Purpose

*Lord, thank You for giving me purpose in life, **for creating me as Your workmanship, with specific work to do**, which You planned in advance. Jesus, Lamb of God, Your sacrifice for me is awesome. Thank You for shedding your blood, so I can be cleansed! Amen.*

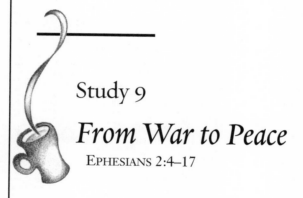

## Study 9

# From War to Peace

EPHESIANS 2:4–17

"She just called," my coworker said, "and they're in a McDonald's on a corner of Tiananmen Square. Something's happening they don't understand . . . looks like war!" A fellow worker in our building had taken a tour group to China, following the footsteps of Lottie Moon, an early twentieth-century American missionary. In Beijing they witnessed the uprising in which a young university student in white shirt and dark trousers faced a large tank from the Chinese army. As they sent news from

China, I felt as if I were there.

A few years before, I'd witnessed people on television tearing down the Brandenburg Gate at the Berlin Wall. This year I've experienced vicariously our American troops' taking Baghdad, tearing down the walls and statues of Saddam Hussein. Have you witnessed enemies confronted or barriers dismantled, in person, on television, or over the Internet? Write in the margin how these experiences touched our heart.

God's purpose for the world is peace, not war. He brings peace to your heart as well as to the world. **Even if you face *physical* war in your own world, you can find *spiritual* peace in Him.**

### Jesus Is Our Peace

Read Ephesians 2:14–17. Who are "the two" in verse 14? Go back to Study 8 (Ephesians 2:8–13). Who were the "circumcised"? What did they call the Ephesians? From what were these Gentile-Ephesians separated? From what were they excluded? To what were they "foreigners"?

Using Ephesians 2:12–13, fill in the blanks: The Gentile Ephesians had been

separate from _____,

excluded from _____ in Israel,

and _____ to the covenants of the promise.

Are the above statements true? Why or why not?

A *Gentile* is anyone not Jewish. The Jewish religious leaders discriminated against any Gentile (called *ethnos*; in English: *ethnic*) or pagan, especially the Ephesians, known for their large temple for the pagan goddess Diana. Paul says Gentiles were separate from Christ, excluded from citizenship in Israel, and foreigners to the covenants of the promise (the covenant God gave the early Jewish Patriarchs, fathers such as Abraham, Isaac, and Jacob, promising His "chosen people" would become a great nation with many descendants).

It's easier to criticize the Jews in Bible times than it is to criticize yourself today. How do you identify Jews (not by circumcision)?

Do you see more prejudice against Gentiles, other ethnic groups, or Jews in today's society?

What other kinds of prejudice do you see?

What kind of stereotyping do you see?

## Knowing God's Purpose

Two thousand years later, we can see the prejudice between the Jews and Gentiles from these verses. Yet God had a purpose, the opposite of prejudice and warring factions between these two groups: He "made the two one and has destroyed the barrier, the dividing wall of hostility." Look carefully at Ephesians 2:14–17. How did He accomplish His purpose? "By abolishing in his flesh the law with its commandments and regulations." Jesus came to fulfill the law and establish a new covenant—a New Testament, or will. *Extra reading:* Hebrews 7:18–19; 9:1,11–28.

The next words are important, summarizing His plan for the Church today: **"His purpose was to create in himself** [that is, Jesus] **one new man out of the two** [all people, Jews and Gentiles], **thus making peace,** and in this one body [the Church] to reconcile both of them to God through the cross, by which he put to death their hostility."

Knowing God's purpose—all people united in one Church with Him as head—what hostility inside *you* does He need to put to death? Remember, His purpose in you is *no hostility.* You're in the process of being sanctified, made pure and blameless in His sight (review Study 2).

The Jews built tremendous barriers of prejudice against the Gentiles. What are your barriers (things that prevent all people joining together to worship God, with Jesus as our head)?

Name a few barriers in your family, your community, or your own heart:

Examine the last few phrases (verse 17) above. From your perspective, who are those who are "near"? Then think about who those are who are "far"—people who are mean? Dirty? Loudmouthed? Ignorant? Different culture/color? Different political party? Estranged family members? Ask God to bring you near Him and them.

Are you willing for God to bring you near those who are far away?

Write Him your promise to move near Him and them:

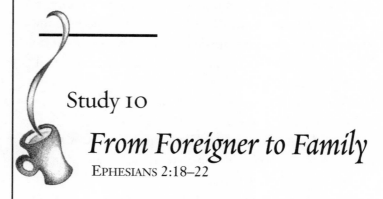

## Study 10

# From Foreigner to Family

EPHESIANS 2:18–22

A HUNGRY WIDOW AND HER DAUGHTER-IN-LAW, LIVING WEST of Baghdad, decided to walk all the way to Israel, where they could find abundant food. The journey on foot was extremely difficult. The older woman became exhausted, asking the younger one to go back home to her people, who may feed her; but the younger woman refused to go. A new believer, she wanted to go to Bethlehem, the mother-in-law's hometown, with her godly mentor. At night under the stars, after each hard day's travel, the older woman told the younger about Jewish culture, helping her to understand how to be accepted among the women there. She shared her wealth of experience. After they arrived, she integrated her daughter-in-law into the culture smoothly, helping the community to admire her and see she was also a godly woman. The older woman was not perfect; she admitted to the Bethlehem women that she was bitter about her husband and two sons' deaths. But her honesty and resourcefulness are still today an example to us. She moved her formerly pagan daughter-in-law from being a foreigner to being a member of the family of God.

You may have recognized this story as the Old Testament account of Ruth and her mother-in-law, Naomi. Do you relate to your mother-in-law (or daughter-in-law) as well as Ruth and Naomi did? My purpose for today's study is that it 1) **relates to the Church of God** and 2) **relates to *you*, touching your heart in a personal way**.

If you have a loving relationship with your mother-in-law/daughter-in-law, stop now and thank God for her. Write your prayer here:

If you don't have a loving relationship with your mother-in-law, list a few ideas of ways to improve your relationship:

If you don't have a mother-in-law/daughter-in-law, ask God to give you a loving relationship with another specific family member.

Pray now that God will give you renewed love for her. Write your prayer here:

*Friend to Friend*

My friend Tricia says if the average woman hears her mother-in-law's moving next door, she'd feel a sudden call to the mission field! You may not have a perfect relationship with your mother-in-law, but you must admire the way Naomi nudged Ruth to be a member of the family instead of feeling shunned as a foreigner. You must also admire Ruth as she humbly obeyed her mother-in-law, worked hard for her, and followed her advice.

## Who Are Your "Foreigners"?

Paul advises those who are in the family and those who're not: "For through him we both have access to the Father by one Spirit. Consequently, you are no longer foreigners and aliens, but fellow citizens with God's people and members of God's household, built on the foundation of the apostles and prophets, with Christ Jesus himself as the chief cornerstone. In him the whole building is joined together and rises to become a holy temple in the Lord. And in him you too are being built together to become a dwelling in which God lives by his Spirit" (Ephesians 2:18–22).

I'm glad God inspired Paul to write these words. They help me, a Gentile—an original ethnic—to know I'm accepted as a fellow citizen with others—of Jewish heritage or otherwise—who are *completed* members of the family. Aren't you glad you don't have to be a foreigner and an alien?

Have you ever felt like a foreigner, perhaps after you've moved to a new area or church? Write how you felt if you were misunderstood, alone, or excluded:

Share with your study friend.

If you don't have a friend to join you in this study, you may feel like a foreigner now. If so, be encouraged. Go to a nearby church and ask the pastor or a women's leader how to meet godly friends.

Now I'm not short and green with glazed, bulging eyes, but at times I've felt like an alien. Haven't you? **You know the hurt of not being accepted. We all do**. It's common practice to shun folks who don't look or act as you do. What a relief to find acceptance from friends and family, as God promises! **Only through the Holy Spirit can you and I be bound as one spiritual family with complete access to God!**

Notice the progression in verse 19: from citizens (public) to family (personal), members of God's household.

## You Are His House

If you're a Christian, you are a part of His house, which has a foundation, a cornerstone, and bricks. What two sets of people defined the foundation for you? Who serves as a strong cornerstone for you to lean on? What holds you, a brick, along with other Christians, in place?

Eugene Peterson paraphrases in *The Message*: "That's plain enough, isn't it? . . . This kingdom of faith is now your home country. . . . You belong here, with as much right to the name Christian as anyone. God is building a home. . . . **he's using you, fitting you in brick by brick** . . . .We see it taking shape day after day—a holy temple built by God" (Ephesians 2:19–21). With a foundation of Old Testament prophets and New Testament apostles, Jesus as the cornerstone, and the Holy Spirit as mortar holding us all together, you are now a part of something big!

In the space provided, draw a simple house, with the foundation of two parts, a large cornerstone, and individual bricks that go up to the roof. Fill in each section with information from today's study.

## A Prayer of Purpose

*Lord, help me to know I'm home.* **I accept that I am a member of the family** *with all other believers, held together by Your Spirit.* **Help me to find my purpose** *as a part of Your holy temple—thankful for the foundation and resting on the Cornerstone. Amen.*

# Unit 3

# *Lord,*

## Teach Me

### ... My Heritage

DO YOU KNOW ANY FRIENDS OR FAMILY WHO DON'T KNOW JESUS as personal Savior? Have you pondered why some people "get it" and some don't? Remember, God's purpose is that we may know the mystery of God, namely Christ, where all the treasures of wisdom are hidden (Colossians 2:2–3).

**As you learn about His love, His purpose for your life becomes clear.** Ephesians 3 teaches that, as part of your life's purpose, God intends you to hear his call, unite with the family of God, and accept the *truth of the treasure*. Sound like a good idea? Turn the page and discover it!

For this reason, Paul was prisoner—
Suff'ring he'd embrace
For the sake of you and others
Given God's good grace.

Mystery seen in God's Word
And understood by all;
Through the Spirit, prophets and
Apostles heard His call.

And specific is this mys'try—
Promise to them all:
Preach the gospel to the gentiles;
Social barriers fall!

Here we are, in Him united:
Earth and heav'n above.
Every family, named for God, can
Bow their hearts in love.

Knowing Him, abundant, able—
Giving more than we
Could ever hope or ask or think.
Glory to Jesus be!

Study 11

# Passing Along the Mystery
### EPHESIANS 3:1–7

ONE SUNDAY MY DAUGHTER PATSY AND I EXPERIENCED A "holy coincidence." I was tired after working all week, cleaning house all weekend. After lunch Patsy said, "Mom, you know, tonight is the dress rehearsal for the Christmas pageant. I need a shepherd's costume by 4:00." I looked up from the dirty dishwater in the kitchen sink. "Patsy, it's two weeks until the pageant. I'll have your costume ready then."

"But, Mom!" she whined, "Mrs. Franklin said costumes must be ready today!" I looked toward heaven. "Lord, deliver me from making a shepherd's costume today," I whispered with a weary sigh.

"C'mon," I said in a moment, drying my hands. "Let's look in the fabric closet in the hall." Just as I suspected, we had nothing suitable. A pink-and-white flannel, a polka-dot broadcloth, a psychedelic-green polyester—nothing for a shepherd.

"Mom, Mrs. Franklin says it's easy. Plain blue cloth, stitched in a square, sewed up the side with loose arm openings, a boat neckline, both shoulders sloping down to the sleeves—oh, yeah, blue rope around a blue scarf, to look like an Arab shepherd."

"Easy for her to say," I mumbled. Then I remembered something. At the beginning of the school year I'd found a piece of blue cloth in my classroom. With a price tag attached, it was folded in a bag, which I'd placed on the "lost and found" table outside my room. It remained there for months, until one day we cleaned up, placing everything in my bottom file drawer, out of sight. Maybe if I started sewing immediately, I could whip that piece of cloth into a half-decent shepherd costume by late afternoon.

I called the school secretary to get her key; Patsy and I went over, unlocked my room, and there in the bottom drawer was the blue cloth. Inside the bag was a perfectly-shaped shepherd's costume: sewn in a square—hanging exactly at Patsy's feet—loose arm openings, boat neckline, both shoulders sloping down to the sleeves. In the bottom of the bag was a miracle: a smaller piece of blue fabric perfect for a head covering, and two pieces of rope, which fit as a belt and a headband over the scarf/covering—and, of all things—in blue to match the costume!

### The Mystery of the Gospel

How did God accomplish that miracle? Had a Home Economics student sewn the costume and left it for me to find months later? Or did God sew the costume for me that afternoon, out of His compassion for me, a tired mother who prayed for deliverance? I don't know. I know only that He is able to do it, either way! God had given me His grace, insight into His mysteries I'd never recognized before. Life is more than physical; "through His power," **a spiritual dynamic touches all of us**, especially if we are Christians.

Read the following sentence, then fill in the blanks with words found in Ephesians 3:1–7.

God "administered," or wisely gave, grace to _____ _____ for _____ . . . through _____.

Paul explains in Ephesians 3:1–7. Read this passage now.

Like Edna, have you experienced a "holy coincidence"? What happened?

## God's Economy of Grace

Paul uses the word *grace* twice. Grace is **G**od's **R**iches **A**t **C**hrist's **E**xpense.

> **To whom** did God give grace? (verses 1, 7)
>
> **For whom** did God give grace to Paul? (verse 1)
>
> **Through what** did God give grace? (verse 7)

Paul, *to* whom God gave grace, *through* the working of God's power, received it *for* the *Gentiles*, the pagan outcasts! In a greater sense, he received grace to pass along to *you* so you— and all people—can believe Jesus is your Savior, sacrificing Himself as an atonement (*propitiation*, if you want to use the fancy word!), so you can escape punishment, living eternal life in heaven!

Examine the phrase "*administration* of God's grace"; the first Greek word carries the idea of "religious stewardship," "wise giving," or "managing with economy." God doesn't waste anything on you. He economically plans, *working His power* in you in just the right way. **He uses—for His glory— every experience He allows in your life.**

How does He do it? Beats me! It's a mystery of spiritual, not physical, proportions: Gentiles (who know little about Moses' law) become, through the gospel, supernatural heirs with Israel (who've kept the law all their lives). We're members together of one body (the family of God). **We're "children . . . heirs of God and co-heirs with Christ"** (Romans 8:17). We share together in the promise in Christ Jesus because we have a spiritual relationship with a personal Savior!

## A Prayer of Purpose

*Lord,* **forgive me when I'm so bound by physical rules that I can't see Your spiritual power.** *Help me, like Paul, to accept the mystery of the Gospel: Jesus died for me. I praise You for grace that makes me heir to the family inheritance: eternal life. Amen.*

## Study 12

# *Personal Access to the Mystery*

EPHESIANS 3:8–12

DR. BILL CAUSEY TELLS A STORY CALLED "AT MIDNIGHT." He'd driven miles from home to lead a revival, returning late that night because his wife was sick. On a deserted highway near the town of Midnight, his car broke down—at midnight. Getting out, he saw, about a quarter-mile down the road, the silhouette of a pickup truck. He walked to it and tapped on the door.

A giant man in a cowboy hat and boots sat up and then got out, towering over Causey, who says, "He was large enough to make me feel like a child. He gave me a lift to a service station, where we sought water out back, alerting every dog in town. Finally, after getting enough water for my car, we got it started, and he offered to follow me to a truck stop in the next town to make sure my car was all right. In a truck stop at 3:00 A.M., I bought us two cups of coffee and asked him if he knew the Lord. He said 'no,' so I asked him if he'd like to, and he said he would—very much like to. I led Him to Jesus, and we prayed aloud with truckers coming and going around us.

"When I asked where he was going, he replied, 'I *was* headed to a place in Arkansas to take my life with the gun I have with me.' I then asked, 'Where are you going now?' He replied, 'Back home to my wife and kids, now that this has happened.' The last time I saw him, he was happily headed for home, taking the New Testament I'd given him."

## Share God's Unsearchable Treasures

A man, poor in spirit, found the **unsearchable riches of Christ** because of a "coincidental" car breakdown and a Christian willing to share the treasure! God has chosen people like Bill Causey to share the gospel since Paul's day. Read Ephesians 3:8–9. *Extra reading on God's hidden treasures*: 2 Corinthians 2:9–10, Isaiah 65:24, Psalm 25:14, John 16:12–13; Colossians 2:2–3, Isaiah 45:3; 1 Corinthians 4:1–5.

Do you, like Paul, feel you are "less than the least of all God's people?" Why or why not?

According to Ephesians 3:8–12, although you may not feel worthy or prepared, what does God's grace enable you to do?

1.

2.

Scripture contains many references to the *mystery* of our Lord, who says, "Call to me and **I will answer you and tell you great and unsearchable things you do not know**" (Jeremiah 33:3). In today's study you have a two-pronged scriptural mandate: 1) preach to the Gentiles the unsearchable riches of Christ and 2) make plain to everyone the administration of this mystery. If you're a Christian, one purpose for your life is evangelistic: *preach*, or tell people how Christ enriches your life. Another purpose is educational: *make plain* the administration of this mystery (see Study 11). Verses 8 and 9 tell you how to direct your preaching and teaching: *to the Gentiles* and *to everyone*. You are not only to be "religious" among your Christian friends, but also are to share naturally with those who are different and be alert in *every* situation to tell *everybody* about Jesus.

How does your lifestyle reflect the inclusion of everyone?

In the last month, how have you related or witnessed to those of other faiths?

Other races?

Other age groups?

Other economic levels?

## *Approach God's Eternal Purpose*

The next words expand my world! Paul explains: "His intent was that now, through the church, the manifold wisdom of God should be made known to the rulers and authorities in the heavenly realms, according to his eternal purpose which he accomplished in Christ Jesus our Lord. In him and through faith in him we may approach God with freedom and confidence" (Ephesians 3:10–12).

According to these verses, through what living institution should God be made known? Through the Church: that is, the living body of God's people. **That's you—and all other Christians around you!** What a challenge!

Do you know Christians who do not accept the challenge of making God known?

According to God's eternal purpose, to whom should you make known the things you know about God (the wisdom of God)?

How are you different from them?

What can you do to encourage other Christians—and to encourage yourself—**on purpose**, to accept the challenge from God's word?

Now, here's the *hard* part: God calls you to accept His challenge, living His purpose for your life: bring glory to Him by telling and teaching others that true riches come from God. **He commands your life's purpose to originate in Him, come alive in your relationship with Him, and flow out to others through Him-in-you.**

And here's the *exciting* part: God's purpose *for you* is far greater than you imagine: once you know His purpose, He expects you, part of His Church, to live with enough freedom and confidence to demonstrate His wisdom to the rulers and authorities in heavenly realms!

**Are you giving God elbow room to work in your life?** Start today looking for the element of surprise, in moments when He reveals the mystery of Christ in you.

Dear One, answer the question Bill Causey asked the trucker: Where are you going now?

## A Prayer of Purpose

*Lord, forgive me for not understanding the mystery of grace. I do call on You now. As I draw near, tell me the unsearchable riches of Christ. Help me make it plain to all—in heaven and earth—that* **You are Lord of my life**. *Give me a heart that sees others. Amen.*

Study 13

# Personal Power in My Heart
EPHESIANS 3:13–17A

I'VE TALKED WITH MANY MISSIONARIES WHO SAY, "DON'T PRAY for an easy life for us; pray for courage under fire," or "Pray we'll be faithful to the end, no matter what the cost." I'm mystified by their steady purpose of serving God in spite of persecution and danger. They could pray for protection and luxury, but they have **surrendered to God's will**, to follow Him anywhere—even through danger, suffering, and death— as He accomplishes *His purpose* for the gospel through their suffering. They ask us to pray for their own personal power to follow God's will, regardless of where it leads.

When you are suffering, how do you pray?

Write in the space below a prayer demonstrating your willingness to suffer for the cause of Christ:

## I'll Follow Him Anywhere

A World War II pilot was shot down behind enemy lines in China. Fearing Japanese scouts, he hid his parachute and ran a distance away. Suddenly an Asian peasant jumped out of the underbrush. Not able to tell if he was Japanese or Chinese, the pilot stopped, breathing heavily, on guard. Then the peasant motioned the pilot to follow him. Fearing ambush, the pilot followed, shaking at each turn in the path. Sensing the pilot's fear and unable to communicate in his language, the peasant began humming a tune: "Amazing grace, how sweet the sound, that saved a wretch like me . . ." Recalling the experience after they reached safety, the pilot said, **"I would have followed him anywhere!"**

When you're in danger or suffering, can you follow the sound of God's tune? Under difficult circumstances, can you still sing of God's amazing grace?

Pretending you are the peasant rescuing the pilot, hum "Amazing Grace" as a gift to your study friend. If you know the words, ask her to join in all stanzas you recall. Write below what this experience means to you:

## Don't Be Discouraged

When I fell on ice in February 2004, dislocating my elbow, the "funny bone" pain that didn't let up for hours was not funny. The suffering lasted months, even after surgery and weeks of physical therapy. I admit I prayed a few *whining* prayers! My suffering, however, wasn't for the cause of Christ and can't compare with Christ's suffering in crucifixion. Paul, imprisoned for his faith in Rome, wrote, "I ask you, therefore, not to be discouraged because of my sufferings for you, which are your glory. For this reason I kneel before the Father, from whom his whole family in heaven and on earth derives its name. I pray that out of his glorious riches he may strengthen you with power through his Spirit in your inner being, so that Christ may dwell in your hearts through faith" (Ephesians 3:13–17a).

Look at the most important word in the first phrase: *discouraged*—literally, "away from (*dis*) the heart (*cour*)." Have you ever had a day that just took away your heart to keep on trying?

Write how you felt when you didn't have the heart to go through a painful time:

Share with your study friend.

How did God strengthen you?

Paul was concerned that new Ephesian converts might lose heart, hearing he was imprisoned for his faith. Perhaps they'd be afraid, discouraged about their own future. Instead of calling imprisonment a disgrace or a tragedy, however, Paul says it's "your glory." The Greek word for *glory* here is based on a root word meaning "honor, dignity, or worship." Paul indicates that true inner power enables Christians during tribulation; you can live in dignity—even worshiping in the presence of suffering! *Extra reading*: 2 Corinthians 3:7–18; 4:1–7

## Refine My Heart, O Lord

In *Power Praying*, Jennifer Kennedy Dean quotes Proverbs 17:3: "The crucible for silver and the furnace for gold, but the Lord tests the heart." She says, "Do you see? . . . what a furnace does for gold, God does for the heart. . . . The Messiah will be like a refiner of silver. In the refining process heat is applied. The silver and the impurities separate. The pure silver settles to the bottom and the impurities rise to the top where they can be skimmed off."

**God removes your impurities as He refines you.** Isaiah says God refines, testing you in "the furnace of affliction" (Isaiah 48:10). "He will be like a refiner's fire or a launderer's soap. He will sit as a refiner and purifier of silver; he will purify [you] and refine [you] like gold and silver" (Malachi 3:2b–3a).

Paul kneels in obedience to God's will, bowing as he accepts the dignity of the family name, "Christian," and the glorious riches of the Almighty!

## A Prayer of Purpose

*Lord, thank You for power to endure suffering. I praise You for what I've learned through trials. I acknowledge **my purpose in the midst of suffering**: to look for Your strength and power in my inner being, as You dwell in my heart of faith. Come, Lord Jesus. Amen.*

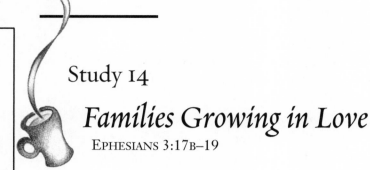

Study 14

# Families Growing in Love

EPHESIANS 3:17B–19

WE ENDED STUDY 13 WITH PAUL PRAYING GOD WOULD strengthen the inner being of new Ephesian Christians. Far away in Rome, Paul must have felt like a mother experiencing empty nest syndrome. He remembered the birth of the Ephesian church and had watched her growing pains.

Though Christian mothers like me hurt when our children suffer, we know that going through the fire strengthens them, and **we can trust God to do what's best**. In 1992 a hospital called to let me know my son had been in an auto accident, breaking a leg and his pelvis in three parts. During those long days in three hospitals in Alabama and Georgia, I prayed for no suffering and complete recovery. Jack hasn't completely recovered (he still walks with a limp), but God has given him "this love of Christ, . . . that surpasses knowledge" to endure.

Not long ago, Jack said, "Mother, my leg pain is nothing, insignificant compared to the joy I have in everyday living. God spared my life; I have a wife who loves me, a beautiful daughter, a good job. Living for Him is the most important thing in my life." Jack, Wendy, and daughter Blakely attend church every week, active in all church events.

My daughter, too, has suffered, with lupus (including asthma, fibromyalgia, an early hysterectomy, chronic pneumonia, and blood clots). When Patsy's doctor predicted tests would show a jalapeno-shaped tumor on her liver as *cancerous*, I spent the night praying against hope that she would be all right. After tests were complete, the specialist told her the tumor was not cancerous! She looks up in hope, thought she still suffers with excruciating arthritis pain at times. During a recent bout with severe pain, she said, "Mom, I've faced death. After that, these pains are nothing. No matter how badly I hurt in the future, I know I can do it. This, too, shall pass." She joyfully teaches first graders, plans Sunday school and Bible school activities, and helps her husband, a minister, with events at church!

Patsy and Jack's suffering has steeled and refined them as strong Christians. I thank God even as I write these words that He's given them inner strength to accept His will, praise Him, and give Christian counsel to others. **Think about what it means to break through hardships and come out on the other side to welcome the fullness of God!**

Describe how you've released your family to God's care:

*Friend to Friend*

Discuss your trust level with a friend.

## Rooted and Established in Love
Read Ephesians 3:17b–19.

Have you ever been to British Columbia, Denmark, or Alaska? I've noticed flowers there, like crocuses or pansies, that live a hardy life even in icy snow. Rooted and established in the cold, they survive better than pampered hothouse plants. Paul knew the Ephesians had been rooted and established in love because he had established the Church there. He'd loved every one of them and prayed they had the power not to wilt at the first adversity. He knew they were saints with as much credibility and sanctification before God as a high priest in Jerusalem! *Review sanctification, Study 2.*

Are you a saint? Are you willing to be one, if God sanctifies or refines you?

What's Paul's prayer purpose? That the saints would have power to do three things:
1) to grasp how vast Christ's love is,
2) to know this love that surpasses knowledge, and
3) to be filled to the measure of all God's fullness.

Circle below traits of sainthood (what makes one a saint):

• Good things I do every day, such as taking food to hungry families
• Generous giving to my church and other good causes
• Unselfishness; putting others first
• Accepting grace from God
• Being saved, through relationship with Christ

Are you afraid if you accept sainthood and allow God to refine you, you'll suffer or lose your "*way-cool*" status with non-Christian friends?

Discuss with your study friend why you may be afraid to break through the pain and accept sainthood.

## Given the Measure of Faith

One thing that makes us *sanctified saints* is total saturation with God's love and grace. Paul prays his Christian friends will be able to grasp the vast dimensions of Christ's love. He points to *the* measure, not *a* measure of God's fullness. Have you ever longed to have the strong faith someone else has or wished for never-doubting faith? Paul indicates you have the same measure of fullness that everyone else has . . . not *a* measure (that is, each one with a different level of faith), but *the* measure, the same level given equally to all. **How you exercise the faith God gives you is up to you.** You have it, Sanctified Saint! Act on it!

## Study 15

# *An Able Family Forever*

### EPHESIANS 3:20–21

AS A NEW CHRISTIAN, STANDING ON THE SIDEWALK IN front of McGee's Drug Store in my hometown, I watched a boy eating an ice cream cone. On that hot July day my thirst for the cool, creamy ice cream was overwhelming. I had one problem: I didn't have a nickel, the cost of one-scoop cones in that day. Longingly I watched as the boy smiled at me and licked his ice cream. Then I thought, "I'm a Christian now! I can pray in a new way. God will hear me!"

"Lord, I want a nickel; please give me a nickel or five pennies; either way, give me enough to buy an ice cream cone," I prayed with my head bowed.

Whispering "Amen," I opened my eyes and saw a nickel between my feet.

Did some generous Christian see a little girl praying and lay a nickel at my feet? Did the boy with the ice cream take pity and donate it? Did God Almighty zap a nickel to the sidewalk in His miraculous power? I don't know.

I've wondered why God answered such a selfish prayer

from a girl. I believe He did it to teach me the power of prayer at the very beginning of our personal relationship, helping me trust Him for bigger things, showing me He's able to do anything I ask, and immeasurably more!

## God's Power Astounds

Often I've prayed for miracles in my family. One night my husband had a toothache. All looked well—no cavities, no swelling—but a stabbing, aching jaw kept him awake all night. (And me, too. If you're married, you know exactly what I mean!) I applied hot compresses, an ice pack, aspirin, and numb-gum-gel, in various stages of the night. Nothing helped. Then I prayed: *Lord, I'm exhausted. I love him so much . . . please take him out of his misery, NOW.* Immediately my husband slumped in the bed. I called his name. No answer. He was dead to the world.

Dead to the world? Yipes! I checked under his nose for breath. Yes. I listened to his heart. Yes. Thank goodness, God had taken him out of his misery, but not all the way to heaven. When he awakened the next morning, he said, "I've had the best night's sleep I've ever had. I'm really refreshed. What happened?"

He and I rejoiced that God is able!

## God's Power Abounds

As I've traveled over this country and around the world, I've found thousands who've told of God's miraculous power. Two women recounted this story: One Christmas Eve in an orphanage, two women listened as a little girl prayed. She believed in God, that He could do more than she could ask. All she wanted for Christmas was the same Christmas gift Mary received: a little baby. The two women looked at each other when they heard the prayer. "Well, dear," they said, "A doll . . ."

"Not a doll," she interrupted. "A real baby."

Heavy-hearted, the two women went to bed. A few hours later they heard a noise at the door. Opening it, they found a live baby on the steps!

Hardly believing their eyes, they presented the baby to the little girl. "It's our Christmas baby, sent from God," they said. They had experienced His power beyond their imagination.

That baby girl grew up loved and comforted by the little girl and the two women. She became God's gift to others; He called her as a missionary.

Write the principles you think are important from the nickel story and the Christmas baby story:

Do you believe power-filled miracles occurred only in the first century to launch the Church? Why or why not?

Do you look for miracles surrounding you? Why or Why not?

Like the women in the orphanage, Paul experienced miracles: the lame walked, demons disappeared, sick people recovered. He says, "Now to him who is able to do immeasurably more than all we ask or imagine, according to his power that is at work within us, to him be glory in the church and in Christ Jesus throughout all generations, for ever and ever! Amen" (Ephesians 3:20–21). As you look at the first three words, who is "*him*"? Whose power is at work within us? In the church? In Christ Jesus? Who works through all generations forever?

**Our awesome God has that power!** If I had all the world's vocabulary, I couldn't describe it. God's power is more—immeasurably more—than I can ask or imagine (some translations say "or think"). Oh, join me now in exalting His glory! Say aloud, "O Lord, Your power and glory are awesome!" Celebrate Him now!

His power works in *your church*—as imperfect as it is! His power works in your child and your grandmother—all generations, as imperfect as they are! And His power and glory continue forever!

## A Prayer of Purpose

*Lord, words can't express how awesome You are! I praise You with my small mind, knowing **You're able to do more than I can ever imagine**. I bow humbly before You, Omnipotent God. May Your power fill my life, my church, and my family forever. Amen.*

# Unit 4

# *Lord,* Help Me Walk with Purpose

IF SOMETIMES YOUR SPIRIT IS DRY, YOU AREN'T ALONE. EVERY Christian has dry spells, like dead bones in the desert. In Ezekiel 37, when God breathed His Spirit into bones, they came alive and started walking around! It can happen to you. **As you surrender to His will, you begin to walk worthy—on purpose!**

Ephesians 4 is the *life purpose chapter*. It explains how, as you discover your purpose, God breathes *new life* into you. You're revved up, alive! The Church of the living God comes alive, too, as you join other Christians and begin a walk of purpose. Interested in walking worthy? Turn the page and begin!

Walk in Jesus, worthy of calling,
Humble, meek; don't cease.
Patient, tolerant, loving, united
In the bond of peace.

One body, Spirit, Baptism, Faith,
One Lord, and hope of call;
One God and Father, measure of grace . . .
Christ's gifts to us all.

He descended; He ascended
To give these gifts we list:
Apostles, prophets, pastors, teachers,
And evangelists.

Equip the saints, build up the church!
Grow up and unify;
Lay aside your former life;
Don't steal or curse or lie.

Don't give the devil half a chance;
Speak the truth in love.
Mature your faith. Always forgive,
As God forgives above.

## Study 16

# *Prisoners Walking in Unity*

EPHESIANS 4:1–6

AS A TEENAGER I FELT I WAS IN PRISON. MY VERY PROTECTIVE father didn't allow me much freedom. Mother seldom opposed Daddy. I admired a friend's mother, who wore electric-pink hot pants (short shorts), drank martinis, and smoked mini-cigars with long plastic extensions, blowing smoke rings across the room. I remember thinking how glamorous she was compared to my mother in a dull housedress.

As a high school junior, I was tired of being good. Good girls had no fun, I concluded. One day I rode home with two wild girls in my class who had "reputations." Was I cool! We drove to a gas station, and to my surprise, they pulled out a girlie magazine from under the front seat and showed the centerfold to the station owner, a friend of my father! He peered inside, eyeing me in the front seat between them.

Mortified, I promised God that if He'd get me out of that car and keep that man quiet around my father, I'd be grateful for the "prison" He'd placed me in. Since then I've thanked God over and over for my godly parents, grateful for my strict-but-kind dad and a mom who wasn't a smoking, drinking diva in hot pants!

## *Willing Submission, Worthy of the Calling*

Sometimes our prisons are artificial, imposed by outside rules or by protective parents. Sometimes **we Christians submit ourselves willingly as prisoners to serve our Lord in special ways.** In Rome, in prison for his faith, Paul says, "As a prisoner for the Lord, then, I urge you to live a life worthy of the calling you have received. Be completely humble and gentle; be patient, bearing with one another in love. Make every effort to keep the unity of the Spirit through the bond of peace. There is one body and one Spirit—just as you were called to one hope when you were called—one Lord, one faith, one baptism; one God and Father of all, who is over all and through all and in all" (Ephesians 4:1–6).

According to Paul, what are you to do to live a life worthy of God's calling?

1. Be _____ and _____

2. Be _____ bearing with _____

in _____

3. Make every_____

to keep _____

of the Spirit through the _____

Dear child of God, as you cease rebelling—and follow His instructions, not as a grudging prisoner of your Father's rules, but willingly surrendering to obey Him—you'll find the greatest freedom inside His loving, protective arms! You'll live a life worthy of your calling, with a strong purpose: **take *your will* prisoner**; take charge of it! Ephesians 4:1–6 contains clear instructions on how to *insist on His purpose* in your life:

1. Be completely humble and gentle.
    *Easy, right? Riiight.*
2. Be patient, bearing with one another in love.
    *Well, it's hard to bear the "know-it-all" woman at church who irritates me.*

3. Make every effort to keep the unity of the Spirit through the bond of peace.

*I can do that easily, until someone disagrees with me—but how can I keep unity when those young members want to play wild music? Surely the Spirit doesn't enjoy that!*

## Willing Unity, Bonding in Peace

I'll never forget one letter I received when I edited *Royal Service* magazine:

Dear Editor:
This is the worst magazine I've ever read. I used to put up with this, but now I hate the new changes. I hate everything about it. Please cancel my subscription to this awful magazine.
    In the deepest Christian love,
    Your Loving Reader

Do these words reflect a *loving* reader? Christians *in the deepest Christian love* practice unity in a bond of peace. **You can speak the truth in love without hurting feelings** or tearing your church apart (or a Christian editor—I'm glad I received several affirming letters in that day's mail, too!). Paul suggests how to communicate in love: make *every effort* to keep unity and peace.

Select and list the points of unity in the Church: Paul says there is one . . .

1.

2.

3.

4.

5.

6.

7.

How do these apply specifically to your church?

He says there is 1) **one body**, the body of Christ, the Church (that's *your* church, too). There's also 2) **one Spirit**, the *Holy Spirit*, whom you can trust in times of disunity; 3) **one hope**—of eternal life, but also the common hope of the Kingdom of God on earth, born in hearts of people working together in Christian unity. Join fellow Christians in following 4) **one Lord**; encouraging them to exercise their 5) **one faith**, corporate faith in our Lord; then follow faith with 6) **one baptism** to demonstrate your belief; as you obey the 7) **one—and only—God and Father of all**.

What comfort! Your heavenly Father, Protector, and Comforter is "over all, through all, and in all." His sovereignty reigns *over* us; His power works *through* us; and His Holy Spirit dwells *in* us as His corporate Body, the Church.

## A Prayer of Purpose
*Sovereign Lord, **I surrender to Your will**, as Your obedient prisoner, to serve You daily. Forgive me when I strain against Your yoke. Let me serve You cheerfully, joining others to unify the Church through the bond of peace. May we know You as Father of all! Amen.*

Study 17

# Captives Walking with Gifts
EPHESIANS 4:7–10

ON A PLANE, I SAT DOWN NEXT TO A MAN WHO SHARED THAT he was returning home for his mother's funeral. "I hate flying," he said. "The Bible says, '*Lo* I am with you always,' but Jesus doesn't promise He'll be with us up high!" I shared with him how I love to fly, enjoying flying into New York just after 9-11, and staying near the Maryland postal facility a few days after anthrax had been discovered there. I trust God absolutely when I'm in the palm of His hand. If He chooses to take me to heaven from an airplane, then that's within His will to do so. (It's probably a better way than some others I can think of that involve years of suffering.) A long time ago, I promised God He could lead me any way He wanted, and I would follow. I've had moments of hesitation and fear, but He's proved that He is faithful to bless me.

Before we finished that flight, the mourning son knew he'd meet his mother in heaven someday, and he relaxed for the rest of the trip in God's comfort. He said, "I feel like God's captured my heart and lifted it up beyond where I could see. I know one day I'll go even higher!"

## Captured in Grace

Has God captured your heart and lifted it high? Read Ephesians 4:7–10. **God has given you the greatest gift,** found in verse 7: **His grace,** or overflowing kindness, merciful blessing. Paul quotes Psalm 68:18, which speaks of Jesus' power to captivate. When He came down to earth—the lower, earthly

Check below any good/
bad gifts, pettiness, or criti-
cisms you hold on to:
□ Fear of flying
□ Nagging my husband
□ Complaining
□ Deaths in the family that
    were unfair
□ Talents I don't use
□ Illness that robs me of
    health
□ Musical, sewing, home-
    making skills I could
    share but don't
□ Loss of job, family mem-
    ber, friend
□ Quirky personality
□ Selfishness
□ Family friction
□ Church attendance out
    of guilt
□ Resentment
□ Arguments
□ Fruits of the Spirit I can't
    share
□ My secret
□ Other:

What will you do about
releasing these for God's
purpose?

regions—He returned to heaven *with us trailing along behind Him*, holding the gifts He and only He could give us.

Psalm 68:18 continues by telling us who those men (and women) were: "even the rebellious—that you, O LORD God, might dwell there." Did you catch the last phrase? The reason God came down to earth was that He might dwell in your heart. Even when you're petty, rebellious, and complaining—when things don't go right—your Lord, who fills the whole universe, gives you gifts, *inviting you to follow Him toward heaven.*

Jesus was the firstfruit; we follow Him in resurrection from death into life (1 Corinthians 15:20–23) and *we become heirs together* . . . in Christ's promise of eternal life (Ephesians 3:6)! *Extra reading*: Exodus 23:19, 1 Corinthians 15:12–28

## *Holding Gifts of Purpose*

Have your surrendered absolutely to His will, or do you stand like a shopper, holding all the gifts He's given you as close as possible, unable to let them be used by anyone, even God Almighty? You may have talents, skills, or even the "spiritual gift of criticism" that's hard to let go. (One of my friends has the gift of criticism, but it's not very spiritual!) Does one of the gift-bags you clutch say "Too Many Low Times"? or "Too Much Humbling, Lord"? Does one say "What are You Doing with My Life?"

**God has a purpose for all gifts**, spiritual and physical: talents, skills, and characteristics that belong to us, that make up our personalities, our total selves. On purpose, sit down and sort them. Then *let all those gift bags go*; be willing to use the good ones to help others and release the bad ones to Him. "Praise be to the Lord . . . who daily bears our burdens" (Psalm 68:19).

Jesus said, "Blessed are the poor in spirit . . . the meek" (Matthew 5:3, 5), but do you feel sometimes you are going through too many low times? Has God given you too much humbling, keeping you low? Give your feelings to Him now.

*Lord, **without complaint**, **I surrender**. You're in charge of my life. Show me my purpose; lead me in grace, perfectly apportioned. I adore You, Lord; **capture my heart anew**. May I always be captive to Your will, using gifts You've given me to serve You. Amen.*

## Study 18

# *Christians Walking Together*

EPHESIANS 4:11–16

I KNEW GOD HAD CALLED ME TO BE A TEACHER. I'D taught Sunday school for fourteen years, and was then teaching adult women how to do missions. I'd agreed to visit a church near my workplace, but that night I got lost. "Why did I agree to teach this handful of women?" I thought. "On this cold night nobody'll come."

I taught with as much enthusiasm as I could, but few women seemed interested. They munched on snacks, glancing my way, but I felt I was wasting my time. After the meeting, one young woman remained. "I enjoyed what you said," she said. "God's called me here to spark interest in what He's doing. They don't know what I know," she whispered, as if God's secret was between us.

I've since been ashamed of my discouragement that night. Susan Beddingfield has become a charming friend. That women's group has come alive with her leadership, and she's started missions organizations for children the ages of her four girls!

I'm excited now when I think of that cold night. So what was wrong with me then? Why didn't I experience joy using my God-given gift of teaching? No matter what you know intellectually, **sometimes your purpose in spiritual matters will fade until you mature in Christ**.

In Study 17 you examined the pettiness of the human spirit that refuses to be happy with God's grace and gifts. In this study you'll explore how, after putting aside your control syndromes, surrendering totally to your Lord, and becoming His captive, you'll *walk with joy and purpose toward God's aim* for your life.

Sometimes, even when you're surrendered to His leadership, determined to follow Him, you may lose heart, resent other Christians, or *forget the gift* God's given you. You may struggle on a slow walk with other Christians toward spiritual maturity.

Have you experienced fighting Christians, hurting pastors, or split church fellowships?

Describe your hurt about a church situation:

Share your answers with
your study friend.

Fill in the blanks:

I'm sometimes jealous of the gifts God has given to
_____.

It bothers me when I see _____ performing at church.

I wish every Christian were as faithful as _____.

I admire _____ for the way he/she serves as a (n) _____.

I think my gift is to serve Christ as _____ _____.

## Serve in Christ

Paul says, "It was he [Christ] who gave some to be apostles, some to be prophets, some to be evangelists, and some to be pastors and teachers, to prepare God's people for works of service, so that the body of Christ may be built up until we all reach unity in the faith and in the knowledge of the Son of God and become mature, attaining to the whole measure of the fullness of Christ. Then we will no longer be infants, tossed back and forth by the waves, and blown here and there by every wind of teaching and by the cunning and craftiness of men in their deceitful scheming. Instead, speaking the truth in love, we will in all things grow up into him who is the Head, that is, Christ. From him the whole body, joined and held together by every supporting ligament, grows and builds itself up in love, as each part does its work" (Ephesians 4:11–16).

In verses 11–16 above, select five gifts (or positions) of service God gives. As He calls certain ones to be 1) apostles, 2) prophets, 3) evangelists, 4) pastors, and 5) teachers, we build up the body of Christ, the Church.

*Extra reading about spiritual gifts*: 1 Corinthians 12:1–11

## Grow Up in Christ

Paul says, "In all things grow up"! How will you know you're a mature Christian? Paul indicates these steps to maturity:

You reach **unity in the faith**. Crafty, scheming people can't destroy your faith. Uniting with other church members, refusing to argue among yourselves like squabbling children, you exhibit spiritual maturity that stands against deceit. You're not fooled by **false leaders** or Satan.

You reach **unity in knowledge of the Son** of God. Agreeing on solid doctrine based on God's Word, refusing to be tossed and turned by every wind of teaching, you demonstrate you're no longer an infant. You've grown up in knowledge of Christ, your church's Head. You're not fooled by **false doctrine**.

You reach **maturity in your measure of fullness** of Christ. Accepting His *full leadership*, you show maturity by doing your work—what He's called *you* to do. Others can measure your fullness-of-Christ by the way you work in unity, speaking the truth in love. You're not fooled by **shallowness and fear**. You accomplish goals, as His Spirit indwells you, fulfilling His purpose in your life.

In Rick Warren's book *The Purpose-Driven Life*, he lists five areas for service: worship, ministry, evangelism, fellowship, and discipleship. Pray now, asking God to show you how to fulfill His intended purpose through you in each of these areas.

How is God nudging you to serve in these areas?

Worship

Ministry

Evangelism

Fellowship

Discipleship

List below an overall plan of action for change:

Does God intend you to be a selfless *change agent* for good in your church, supporting others as *a ligament in the Body of Christ*? The work will take humility and spiritual maturity, accomplished only in God's power. **Don't lose your purpose.**

## A Prayer of Purpose

*Lord, may I never be jealous of God's gifts to others. Help me not to be an infant, tossed by the waves, blown by every wind of teaching and deceitful scheming. May I always speak the truth in love.* **Help me to be a supporting ligament in my church**. *Amen.*

## Study 19

# Newness Walking Without Oldness

EPHESIANS 4:17–24

I WAS A MEAN LITTLE GIRL FOR AS LONG AS I CAN REMEMBER. One summer I knocked my brother Jim's front teeth out with a baseball—on purpose. I also pinched my cousin Lamar until his arm was purple because he wanted to play with the older cousins. I stabbed a classmate with a pencil and another with a piece of glass. A sneaky child, I remember hiding pills my parents asked me to take. It's no secret that by the time I was eleven, I held a lot of sin in my heart. But Christ enabled me to be forgiven and then forgive—to lay aside the jealousy and meanness, as I accepted Him into my heart one night following an invitation at Vacation Bible School that morning.

My "old self" was pretty nasty. Do you have an old self? How often do you let the *oldness* sneak back in to the *newness of life* you've found in Christ? Read Ephesians 4:17–24.

Like Edna, were you once a mean child or rebellious teen? Explain:

Discuss with your study friend how you have changed.

Did the change come with Christ in your heart?

## *Toss the Rot! Renew Your Mind*

*The Message* paraphrases Paul: "I insist—and God backs me up on this—that there be no going along with the . . . empty-headed, mindless crowd. . . . that's no life for you. . . . everything—and I do mean everything—connected with that old way of life has to go. It's rotten through and through. Get rid of it! And then take on an entirely new way of life—a God-fashioned life, a life renewed from the inside and working itself into your conduct as God accurately reproduces his character in you."

What are the main points in verses 17–24?

1. You must *not* live as non-believers, separated from God because of their *ignorance* in the dark.

2. The longer they live without Him, the *more insensitive* they become to His call; they grow more and more sinful.

3. *You have learned better* than that.

4. Take off all that meanness, sneakiness, and anger.

5. Put on a new outfit! **A good attitude will emerge from your mind.**

6. Your *new self* now realizes you were created like God, and *you become truly good* and holy.

What does God mean by "Put off your old self. . . . Put on the new self"?

Personally, how can you do that and stick to that purpose?

The Greek word translated "are darkened" (verse 18) indicates *shadiness* or *blindness*. Have you ever noticed that unchurched people are often blind to truths you recognize? Jesus says, "A man who walks by day will not stumble. . . . It is when he walks by night that he stumbles, for he has no light" (John 11:9–10). He also says, "I have come into the world as a light, so that no one who believes in me should stay in darkness" (John 12:46). Good news! God doesn't want you to stay in sinful darkness, shady dealings, or blind living. He wants you to follow His light. "I am the light of the world. **Whoever follows me will never walk in darkness**, but will have the light of life" (John 8:12). *Extra reading about blindness/darkness:* Acts 13:6–12.

### It's Not Too Late! Walk in Light

Jesus warned His disciples, "You are going to have the light just a little while longer. **Walk while you have the light, before darkness overtakes you.** The man who walks in the dark does not know where he is going. Put your trust in the light while you have it, so that you may become sons of light" (John 12:35–36). Let in the Light, in newness of life now, without delay. **And don't let the "oldness" back in!** Make every moment of light count—eternally, **on purpose**. (You'll find more about darkness in Study 22.)

### A Prayer of Purpose

*Lord, I now take off my old, corrupt self and put on my new, holy self. I desire righteousness, not lust, futility, ignorance, and separation. Help me not to be insensitive to you, but starting today, to **follow the Light of the World with a new attitude**. Amen.*

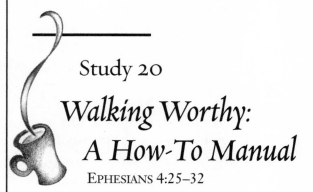

## Study 20

# Walking Worthy: A How-To Manual

EPHESIANS 4:25–32

LEARNING TO WALK IS AN AWKWARD PROCESS. MY GRAND-daughter, Blakely, learned to sit up, pull up, take a step, hesitate, fall, get up again, take a step, then another, toes curled under, slowing trusting . . . and finally, arms waving, she strutted across the room! Similarly, Christians learn to *walk worthy* by slowly trusting, stepping out in faith, stumbling occasionally, and then walking purposefully. God will help you rise from the low, base desires of your carnal nature, leave that *unworthy crawl*, walk worthy in your spiritual nature, and soar with Him.

However, as a baby reverts to crawling even after learning how to walk, even after you become a Christian and know how to walk *worthy*, it's much easier to revert to walking *unworthy*.

## Doin' What Comes Naturally!

As a lazy Christian, you may, like me, revert to natural behaviors: finding excuses not to attend church, neglecting to write encouraging letters, keeping too busy to listen to God's whispers. It's not that you try to be bad; you just lapse into unworthiness, not paying attention to your renewed mind (Study 19).

I once wrote an anonymous letter to a new minister, warning him not to make mistakes in choosing church friends. I did a good job of slandering two people, convincing myself I'd done the right thing. I didn't sign the letter, because I didn't want him to think *I'd* done anything underhanded! Convinced of my noble purpose, I mailed the letter and then forgot it.

Many months later, as I prayed one morning, God reminded me of the anonymous letter, nudging me to tell the minister. "Lord, I couldn't do that. I'll never tell I wrote that letter. Anyway, what good would it do now?"

God's Spirit was unrelenting. I called the church, hoping the minister was out. No such luck; his secretary invited me to come immediately. With trepidation, I entered his office. He welcomed my confession, accepting my motivation. He'd assumed two certain women had written the letter. My letter had thwarted his relationship with them. I deserved the blame, not them, and I told him so. My letter was deceitful, and I learned a lesson on how to walk worthy.

The Ephesians also stumbled in their walk with God. Discouraged, many of them had stopped working. In fear, they hid from their persecutors, even falling into backbiting and lying among themselves. God sent practical encouragement through Paul's letter. Read Ephesians 4:25–32.

Get practical. From verses 25–32, write yourself a reminder list of things to do in order to walk with purpose:

### REMINDER LIST:

*Do:*                                                    *Don't:*

Share your list with your study friend.

Pray over each item on your list, asking God to help you walk worthy.

## God says, Do:

- Stop lying
- Speak truthfully to your neighbor
- Work, doing something useful with your own hands
- Share with needy people
- Speak only what is helpful, to benefit others
- Get rid of *all* bitterness, rage, anger, brawling, slander, and malice
- Be kind and compassionate to one another
- Forgive each other, as Christ forgave you

## God says, Don't:

- Sin in anger; instead, make peace before the sun goes down
- Give the devil a foothold
- Steal
- Let unwholesome talk come out of your mouth
- Grieve the Holy Spirit, with whom you were sealed for the day of redemption

Whew! You can accomplish these only in God's power. He provides a way for you to walk worthy—**on purpose**—through your personal relationship with Him. Ask Him to speak to you about each item above. Don't grieve His Spirit; ask for help in walking worthy, to soar in your Christian walk.

## Don't Give the Devil a Foothold

Paul assumes all of us have anger. How do you handle it?

**1. Aggressors** react to anger in a volatile way. Their first impulse is to steamroll over the other person(s) involved. Their *carnal nature* urges them to lash out verbally or physically.

**2. Repressors** react to anger in a silent way, hiding the anger. Their first impulse is to agree to *anything* to end confrontation. Their *carnal nature* urges them to talk about others behind their backs.

**3. Confessors** are aggressors and repressors who've learned to dissipate their anger in a healthy way. They instantly consult God about their anger, to help them walk worthy. Their *spiritual nature* urges them to speak the truth in love, settling challenges in a spirit of peace.

Examples: **Aggressor/Confessor:** "Lord, You heard what she just said to me. I want to punch her out. Give me patience. Stop my temper. Help me speak kindly. May I walk worthy."

**Repressor/Confessor:** "Lord, You heard what she just said to me. Help me speak up! Give me words to tell her how I feel. Help me bring long-lasting peace between us. May I walk worthy."

## A Prayer of Purpose

*Lord, help me be kind and compassionate to others, giving forgiveness and accepting it, as God forgave me in Christ. May I hold no anger, bitterness, or rage.* **Take away my tendency to slander or hurt others**, *and give me honest work to do for You. Amen.*

# Unit 5

# Lord, I'm Just Like ... My Mother!

YOU WERE BORN IN THE IMAGE OF GOD; THEREFORE, YOU resemble your Father. He created you with an innate longing for Him. To fulfill that longing, your Father wants to live in your heart. **He also wants to see Himself reflected in you, as you purpose to imitate Him** in a daily walk of purity.

Would you like to know what a pure, purposeful walk looks like? Fanny Crosby wrote, "Perfect submission, all is at rest, I in my Savior am happy and blest: watching and waiting, looking above, filled with His goodness, lost in His love." Does perfect submission sound like a good place to be? Ephesians 5 will take you there. Read on!

Children, imitate your God;
Be aroma sweet.
Thank Him, praise Him; don't befriend
Deceivers in the street.

Formerly of darkness,
With the evil deeds of night.
Wake up, sleepers, from the dead:
You're children of the Light.

Don't be foolish, don't get drunk;
Watch the way you walk!
Pledge yourself to Christian friends,
With hymns and praise your talk!

Wives, now listen to your husbands,
Honor—and respecting.
As churches follow Jesus Christ
To Him themselves subjecting.

As Jesus loved His bride, the Church,
Husbands love your wives . . .
Joining them: one flesh and spirit;
Give your very lives.

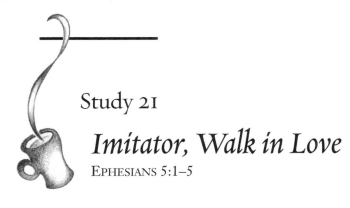

## Study 21

# Imitator, Walk in Love

EPHESIANS 5:1–5

A FAMOUS COMEDIENNE SAID SHE PUT HER ARM IN THE sleeve of her sweater, and her mother's hand came out the bottom! It startled her to realize she looked a little more like her mother every day. When you look in the mirror each morning, do you see your mother?—a sagging chin line, puffy eyes, or wrinkled brow resembling hers? Maybe you recognize her graying hair, beautiful long lashes, or sincere smile. Do you think others see the family resemblance?

## Look Like Your Father

How much do you look like your Father—that is, your Heavenly Father? Do you so imitate His example that He's a part of you, and you become more like Him every day? Can others see the family resemblance, as **you purpose to grow in the family of God**?

Read Ephesians 5:1–5.

From verses 1–5 write things you think God wants you to do:

Do you **think** God really expects you to be *holy*? Why or why not?

Share about family resemblances with your study friend.

Look at the list of sins God tells you to avoid: even a hint of sexual immorality (including dirty jokes and suggestive remarks), impurity, greed, obscenity, foolish talk, or coarse joking. What does God say is wrong with these things, even the mildest form? They are improper, out of place, and idolatrous for God's holy people. Do you worship a flirting, *fun* image of yourself more than you worship Jesus, who "gave himself up for us as a fragrant offering [a sweet gift just for you] and sacrifice to God"? In light of the tremendous pain and suffering He gave, for you, one of His "dearly-loved children" (verse 1), **can't you give up the thing He's calling you to release to Him now?**

It may be a smart remark you're fond of—some "harmless," clever foolishness; something that makes you popular. I've often fallen into *foolish talk* rather than *thanksgiving to God*, and felt sad later that I'd let Him down, considering how much He's given for me.

Though these things are external, they are a reflection of the internal, your heart's core. The world says, "Live a life of flippancy." God says, "Live a life of love."

Team with a study friend to make a practical do-and-don't-list to remind yourselves how to imitate Jesus:

Do:

Don't:

Paul told new Christians in Ephesus to follow what he did. List the names or initials of Christians you'd like to imitate:

## Friend to Friend

Write a letter to at least two of these, to tell them what their good example has meant to you. Then pray that you can be an imitator of Jesus Christ Himself.

While praying to God about us, Jesus said, "Everything mine is yours, and yours mine, and my life is on display in them." That is, the holy character of God that lived in Jesus, is on display in you, dear godly woman. Jesus continues, "They are no more defined by the world than I am defined by the world. *Make them holy*" (John 17:10, 16–17 *The Message*). ["*Sanctify them*" NIV]. Then Jesus tells God about *your* purpose in the world: "In the same way that you gave me a mission in the world, I give them a mission in the world" (John 17:18 *The Message*). **Your mission, should you decide to accept it, is to live as much like Him as possible.** Accept holiness as He gives it. Don't allow even a hint of immorality, impurity, or greed. Fine-tune your character. Be the very best you can be! God has given you His favor. Collect your inheritance in the family of God!

## Take Off the Veil

Here's the best news: we can take off anything that separates us from God. When we lift the veil of deceit, foolish talk, immorality, and greed, then we can, without shame, face our Lord! The closer we get to Him—with no veil, sham, or pretense between us—the more we reflect His *glory*—the radiance of His Holy Spirit dwelling inside us. "And we, who with *unveiled faces* all reflect the Lord's glory, are being *transformed into his likeness* with ever-increasing glory, which comes from the Lord, who is the Spirit" (2 Corinthians 3:18).

## A Prayer of Purpose

*Lord, I want to look just like You.* **Help me be an imitator of God; no one else.** *O, how I want to be Your pure vessel! When I think of Your life given for me, I must give my all for You. Give me purity today—and assurance of my inheritance in heaven. Amen.*

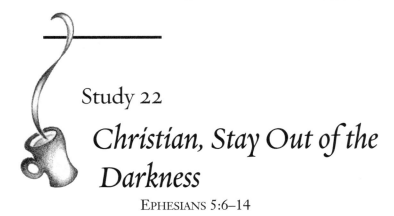

## Study 22

# *Christian, Stay Out of the Darkness*

EPHESIANS 5:6–14

AS A YOUNG CHURCH MEMBER, I TAUGHT A MISSIONS STUDY at our church, which I had done several times before. This time the study book's topic was the occult. Following the study, I said goodbye to my husband, who had to work the night shift, went home, put the children in bed, and went to sleep. I later woke with a start, sitting up in bed. Half asleep, half awake, I saw a dark face on the wall. It said, "If you don't quit preaching against me, I'm going to hurt your children!"

"Preaching?" I thought. "I'm not a preacher. What is this?" Then I heard Jack screaming across the hall. As I hit the light switch in my room, the overhead light blew out. Darkness. Next I hit the switch in the bathroom near my bed. It also flashed and then went dark. I ran to the hall switch. It blew out! Panicking, I ran to Jack's room and turned on the light. He was on the floor, covered with blood. I thought his throat had been cut, because he was red from his mouth to his waist, with blood all over his little baseball pajamas. Trying not to show fear, I took off his pajamas in calm motions and washed his face and chest (and turned on every light in the house!).

Irrational thoughts consumed me: Had Satan thrown him out of bed? Had I dreamed that menacing, three-foot tall, black-shadow face, or was it real? I quickly remembered several verses to pray:

"When I am afraid, I will trust in you. . . . **in God I trust; I will not be afraid**" (Psalm 56:3–4).

"You, dear children, are from God and have overcome them, because the one who is in you is greater than the one who is in the world" (1 John 4:4).

"In all their distress he too was distressed, and the angel of his presence saved them" (Isaiah 63:9).

"Even though I walk through the valley of the shadow of death, I will fear no evil, for you are with me" (Psalm 23:4).

My mind slowly filled with rational thoughts: Jack had fallen out of bed, bumped his nose, and had a nosebleed. The noise of his fall probably caused me to replay in a dream some of the dark ideas from the mission study. Our house had experienced a power surge that blew out the lights.

## Don't Dabble in the Darkness

Nevertheless, I've pledged before God that I'll never dabble in the darkness. Dark powers are real. Deceivers are lurking, Dear Christian. **Wake up and live unswervingly in the light.** Memorize the verses above as your shield against evil.

Absorb these words: "Let no one deceive you with empty words, for because of such things God's wrath comes on those who are disobedient. Therefore, do not be partners with them. For you were once darkness, but now you are light in the Lord. Live as children of light (for the fruit of the light consists in all goodness, righteousness and truth) and find out what pleases the Lord. Have nothing to do with the fruitless deeds of darkness, but rather expose them. For it is shameful even to mention what the disobedient do in secret. But everything exposed by the light becomes visible, for it is light that makes everything visible. This is why it is said: 'Wake up, O sleeper, rise from the dead, and Christ will shine on you'" (Ephesians 5:6–14).

## Wake Up and Step into the Light

Today I read these words in 1 Peter 5:8–11: "Be self-controlled and alert. Your enemy the devil prowls around like a roaring lion looking for someone to devour. Resist him, standing firm in the faith . . . . And the God of all grace, who called you to his eternal glory in Christ . . . will himself restore you and make you strong, firm and steadfast. To him be the power for ever and ever. Amen."

One step to freedom from the bondage of darkness is diagnosing where your darkness is, so you can avoid those areas. Circle those below that give you trouble:

- Reading violent, perverted, or evil materials
- Watching horror movies or the occult
- Being led astray by friends
- Acting out of an evil, uncontrolled heart
- Giving in to depression or feelings of unworthiness
- Lack of confidence in God to protect me
- Allowing bitterness, hatred, and regret to overwhelm me

Isaiah 26:19 also says, "Wake up and shout for joy." Have you shouted for joy in the Lord lately? If not, now is the time to allow Him to help you step totally away from the darkness and into the Light of His joyous love. *Listen to Him now, as He calls you out of darkness into his marvelous light* (1 Peter 2:9).

Perhaps this whole book was written just to refine one dark spot in *your* heart. **God created you to be a child of light**; heaven begins in your heart the day you accept Christ's love, and it goes all the way to the place of perfect light in eternity. (Review Study 19.)

## A Prayer of Purpose

*Lord, protect me from any darkness creeping into my life; help me take a stand against evil.* **I want to live with purpose, as a child of light, in goodness and truth.** *Show me how I can please You, always visible in Your light, reflecting the light to others. Amen.*

Discuss with your study friend.

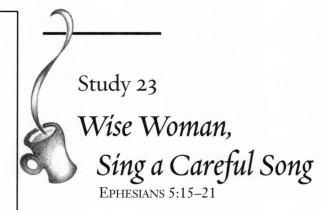

## Study 23

## *Wise Woman, Sing a Careful Song*

Ephesians 5:15–21

From the second grade, my teachers called me careless. I didn't like it, but I had to admit I *was* careless. In math class, I'd hurriedly add 2 + 2 = 3, or I'd finish a hard problem accurately, but forget a decimal point, making the whole answer wrong! In science class I'd do an experiment correctly but fail to turn in my answer sheet.

As an adult I was not much better. I placed this announcement in the church newsletter: "All women of the church, come and bring a friend to the Women on Mission 'Teddy Bear Picnic' Celebration on Tuesday, March 9, at 6:00 P.M. Bring a well-filled basket, and prepare to help with this ice-breaker: tell us why you treasure your favorite teddy bear, and why you treasure the friend you're bringing. Don't forget to bring your fool." Of course, I meant to type "food" instead of "fool," but my carelessness changed the meaning of the announcement!

As Christians, it's important that we not be careless, but live a careful life. Read Ephesians 5:15–21 now.

Are you careless? List a few of your unforgettable bloopers:

Share these with your study friend, if you feel comfortable.

## Living an On-Purpose Life

Living a life with purpose isn't easy. It requires that you be alert, orderly, and sober. God gives you nine commands in these verses.

### 1. Be careful.

As a teenager, I heard this bad advice: "If you can't be good, be careful." God commands that you be both good and careful, not unwisely wasting time or energy on evil, careless habits and actions.

### 2. Make the most of every opportunity.

Which daily opportunities come your way? Do you have a chance to set an example before women spiritually younger than you? Teach children? Witness to non-Christians? Share funds with missions causes? Use talents to benefit your church, home, or community? God asked Moses, "What is . . . in your hand" (Exodus 4:2)? Look at what's at hand today. Then decide—**on purpose**—what to do.

Why are your actions important? Because the days are evil. You can make a difference in an evil world if you stay alert for opportunities.

### 3. Understand the Lord's will.

Verses 15–21 outline things God wills for you. In other studies, we'll see more steps to following His will. Make an effort to understand His will by reading His Word and praying. **Then** *will your own mind and body* **to follow it.**

### 4. Don't get drunk.

There it is, as plain as the label on a bottle of wine: Just say NO.

### 5. Be filled with the Spirit.

Do you have dry spells in which you can't reach God? The answer to that dilemma is to ask God to fill you with His Holy Spirit every morning. He is faithful to His promise, "I will

On a scale of 1 (low) to 10 (high), how do you score on keeping each of these 9 commands?

1.

2.

3.

4.

5.

6.

7.

8.

9.

never leave you or forsake you"—regardless of your fleeting feelings. You ask. He'll indwell.

### 6. Speak uplifting words to one another.

Paul says first: *speak* to one another. If there's anyone with whom you're not speaking, today's the day to seek forgiveness and give forgiveness. Then Paul says *speak in three ways*: with psalms, hymns, and spiritual songs. Cut out profanity; use godly language.

### 7. Sing. Make music in your heart.

How do you make music in your heart? Each person in a different way: some have beautiful voices; some don't. In monotones or golden tones, be sure it's *to the Lord*, as Paul says.

### 8. Give thanks.

Thanksgiving is the language of heaven (Revelation 5:11–13). This command gives you a perfect outline for a prayer of thanksgiving. 1) You thank God 2) praying in the name of the Lord: "O, God, thank You for _____. In Jesus' name, Amen."

### 9. Submit to one another.

For church harmony, you and I are to submit to all church members. Why? Out of reverence for Christ. It doesn't matter how ornery some are. What matters is that you live in harmony to honor your Lord.

## *Be Honor-y to the Ornery*

You can be civil, honoring even the most ornery Christians. Consider what their hidden problems might be. If you have trouble minding what you say, remember: keep those bad *thoughts* away and *sing* spiritual songs!

## A Prayer of Purpose

*Lord, my heart rejoices with joyful songs when I think of Your good-ness.* **Help me live a careful, wise Christian life.** *Protect me in this evil day. I promise You now to stay sober and alert, asking for the indwelling Holy Spirit, giving thanks in Jesus' name. Amen.*

Study 24

# Help Me Walk As a Godly Woman

EPHESIANS 5:22–24

WHEN PATSY WENT TO SCHOOL, THE WOMEN'S RIGHTS movement was in full swing; she even took Women's Assertive-ness Training. Dating men in her classes, she looked for a sensitive man open to a 50/50 marriage. I shared with her a little book suggesting everyone go into marriage expecting a 60/40, not a 50/50, marriage: expect only 40% return for 60% giving. If couples agree, each gives 60%, forgives the little things, and receives a 120% marriage! Impossible? Maybe not, if you count God's way.

## Look at Our Models

I admire wives who spend time on their knees in prayer for their husbands, humbling themselves for the family. They live a life of submission to God first and family second.

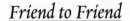
## Friend to Friend

Name some women you admire:

What do you admire about them?

What makes a successful marriage?

Paul says, "Wives, submit to your husbands as to the Lord. For the husband is the head of the wife as Christ is the head of the church, his body, of which he is the Savior. Now as the church submits to Christ, so also wives should submit to their husbands in everything" (Ephesians 5:22–24). Wow!

Do you want to scream, "Paul, you male chauvinist, you're a woman hater!"? Think again.

The relationship between Christ and His Church is mirrored in the relationship between husbands and wives. Look again at verses 22–24: Christ is head of the Church. The Church is His bride, cherished and chosen. The Church is also His body. (A body of believers work together like body parts to grow spiritually. As the Head leads, His Body submits to His leadership; we follow His plan.) Christ the Bridegroom is the

Savior of His bride the Church—saving her from harm, leading her to eternal life. Have you ever wished for Prince Charming to take you in his arms, protect you from harm, and cherish you? For most women, part of their sexual nature is fulfilled through surrender and submission to a virile, loving man.

You'd probably agree, however, that more than physical intimacy, women need love and tenderness. **We want to be loved as Christ loved the Church.** You want your husband to put your wishes above his own, to be willing to die for you. The Prince of Peace was the ideal bridegroom, loving us—the Church—His bride, so much that He gave His life for her. As His bride, you're worthy because He thinks so. He gave His very life for *you*.

In the Garden of Eden, God created order in the family. Adam was created first (Genesis 2:7–8); Eve was created as a helper for him (Genesis 2:18–22). Equal in their relationship to God, nature, and each other, both were created in the image/likeness of God (Genesis 1:27–28). Adam named Eve *Ishsha* (Heb., *woman*), similar to *Ish*, or *man* (Genesis 2:23). She was uniquely *her*, but she was part of *him*. Even her name emphasized their unity. The perfect woman lived with the perfect husband in the perfect home. *Extra reading*: 1 Corinthians 11:11; Colossians 3:9–14

You know the rest of the story: Adam and Eve sinned and had to leave Eden. They accused each other and began an adversarial relationship between women and men that still exists! Adam blamed Eve, complaining that God gave him a flawed woman. To get even, he, as head of the family, decided to take his first-born position seriously, demanding Eve's obedience. In misery, Eve blamed Adam. We argue about the same issues today.

## Look in the Mirror

The more Adam demanded, the more Eve rebelled. God intended for them to be obedient and loving to each other, but because of the Fall, they chafed against the yoke of unity.

Genesis 3:16 paints a sad picture of misunderstanding: "Your desire will be for your husband, and he will rule over you." Did Eve hunger for his touch? She wanted him to adore her; yet he demanded obedience rather than courting her affection. She became manipulative in her rebellion against his demands, and he became angry, continuing the cycle of pain and miscommunication. *Extra reading*: James 4:1–10

In Study 25 we'll discuss a man's responsibility, but for today, let's look at ourselves: what must you do to break the cycle? Every man in your family needs respect (Ephesians 5:33). God created Him to need it, as firstborn. **You can give respect to your husband to break the cycle of disobedience and bickering.**

Consider the men in your family. Is the need for respect a common trait? Explain.

Is your marriage (or that of your parents) a mirror of Christ's relationship with the Church? Why or why not?

Are you weary in obedience? You may think you've already given over 60%, and can't give more. As the prayer of Francis of Assisi asserts, it's in *giving* that you *receive*.

This does not mean, however, you should succumb to any physical or severe emotional abuse. Remember, you are the temple of God and must take good care of His dwelling place. Talk with your study friend or trusted Christian about that topic.

_Lord, as Your Bride, I worship You, surrendering to You, the Bride-groom of the Church. I desire to be obedient to Your will as You lead me. Bring me to right relationship with my husband. **Give me opportunities to show respect and surrender, as You lead.** Amen._

## Study 25

# _Help Him Walk as a Godly Man_

EPHESIANS 5:25–33

AS WE WALK WORTHY OF OUR LORD, FOLLOWING HIS LEAD, we often walk with a partner. I've known the joy of a "two-in-one" marriage. My husband and I were one physically and spiritually. Though no marriage is _perfect_ bliss, we enjoyed each other's company and trusted each other absolutely as we trusted God together. My husband was the best companion, the best lover, the best joke-teller, the best Christian deacon, the best family spiritual leader I could know; he was my best friend. When he went to be with the Lord at age 48, heavenly joy spilled down into my heart. Truly I felt the joy of my "better half," as some say. _Half of me was in heaven_! Miraculously, I never experienced the stages of grief I'd read about. I haven't yet mourned his death, knowing his great joy in heaven! As his wife, I had prayed on my knees for him for twenty-three years, and rejoiced over his spiritual growth day by day. When he went to heaven, he was totally filled with the presence of Jesus, and I rejoiced with him and eagerly await . . . .

List advice Paul gives husbands in Ephesians 5:25–32:

What can you do to encourage your husband to follow these principles for a good marriage?

## Love the Radiant Bride

Paul gives advice to husbands in tender words. Read Ephesians 5:25–33 now. What do these verses tell men to do, for a happy marriage?

**1. Love your wife.**
**2. Follow Christ's example:**
• He loved His bride, the Church, so much he died for her.
• He died so she could become holy.
• She was cleansed by washing with living water though the word (The Bible).
• She was presented to Him as a radiant church, without stain, wrinkle, or blemish, but holy and blameless.
**3. Love your wife as your own body.** (If you love your wife [joined with you as one person], you love yourself. No one hates his own body.)
**4. Care for her;** feed her as Christ does the Church.

5. Remember, **you're members of the same body**.
6. Leave your father and mother; **be united** with your wife.
7. **You two will become one flesh**.
8. Repeat # 1 and # 3: *love your wife* as you love yourself.

Don't you wish every husband could love his wife as Christ loved the Church? Think of what joy we'd have in marriage! No divorce, no fighting, no frustrations. I've heard women say, "It would be easy to be submissive if my husband loved me as much as Christ does! If he always put me first, loved me more than himself, was willing to die for me, wanted me to be washed clean, without stain or wrinkles, never tempted me into sin or anger, why . . . *I'd adore him*! It would be a pleasure to give him the respect he deserves."

In these verses Paul gives only one reminder for a wife: **respect your husband.**

## Respect Him, Worthy or Not

Now here's the catch: **Christ loved the Church *before* the Church loved Him**. "While we were still sinners, Christ died for us" (Romans 5:8). While you were a sinner, He loved you. While you were imperfect, He made it possible for you to be a *perfect* citizen of heaven! While your hands were dirty and your heart was guilty, He saw something worthy in you.

Someone must initiate the cycle of trust and forgiveness. Christ, as our example, began by giving the ultimate sacrifice. How about you? What gift of sacrifice can you give your husband today? Even if he's unworthy, can you initiate mutual submission in your relationship by humbling yourself before him? **Let him see you on your knees, praying for him sincerely, out of love and respect.** Don't wait for him to be perfect before you submit your cooperation; be the first to give honor, inviting his love for you in return.

*Friend to Friend*

## A Prayer of Purpose

*Perfect Bridegroom, thank You for dying for my husband and me. May I be Your radiant, submissive bride.* **Give me wisdom to encourage him to walk worthy,** *as I pray for him daily. Lord, help me to walk worthy, without sin, anger, or a disobedient spirit. Amen.*

# Unit 6

# Lord,

## I'm a Woman
## of Purpose

LIVING A LIFE OF PURPOSE IN THE FAMILY OF GOD IS NOT EASY. You need armor because Christians are at war. Shortly after Creation, the rebellious angel Satan summoned his troops to attack those living in God's will and purpose. Because of evil, God banished Adam and Eve from Eden. Today we've inherited their tendency for evil; we even join in a *family* feud from time to time!

So are we inheritors of conflict, defeat, and death without hope? No! **God has given you the family armor, and you can use it with purpose**. Turn the page, look in Ephesians 6 and find out how to use it!

Kids, obey your parents daily,
And your life is long.
Fathers, do not cause them anger,
When you know it's wrong.

Servants, be kind to your masters;
Work for God, not men.
Bosses, kindness to employees
Blesses work they're in.

Build up power in the Lord
And in His strength and might;
Satan's schemes will fall, in failure—
If you stand and fight.

Buckle up with truth and right—
With peace upon your feet.
Shield yourself with faith, and Satan's
Arrows won't be fleet.

On your head salvation's helmet;
Lift the Spirit's sword!
The holy word of God brings peaceful
Comfort from the Lord.

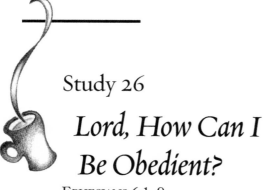

Study 26

# Lord, How Can I Be Obedient?

EPHESIANS 6:1–9

IN THE NINTH GRADE MY HISTORY TEACHER, CALLED "THE Boring Madam X," assigned homework pages and then read—word-for-word—those same pages the next day in class. She often walked out of the room, and chaos followed. I sat in front of "Fonnie," who often whacked me on the head with his math notebook. Once when Madam X left the room, I felt the usual crack on the head. As Fonnie laughed with a friend behind him, I picked up my giant history book and whammed his head as hard as I could! Revenge felt good . . . until I realized Madam X was looming over me. Ushering me to the principal's office, she said, "This young lady is extremely disobedient." Scowling through her horn-rimmed glasses, she said, "Edna, you know our class rule is 'No Misbehavior.'"

Stunned, I almost answered, "Well, you could've fooled me!" but I'm glad I kept quiet. Later the principal talked with me, believed my story of Fonnie's harassment, and helped me learn a good lesson about obedience. **It is *my* responsibility to be obedient, not the responsibility of authority figures or peers.**

## It's All in the Family

As years passed, I've wondered why children take delight in disobedience. Teens consider obedient ones "squares," "dweebs," or "geeks" that don't have any fun. Even adults struggle against urges to disobey rules. Read what God says about obedience in

Ephesians 6:1–9.

From verses 1–9, list two commandments for each of the following:
Children:


Fathers:


Slaves:


Masters:


These verses admonish four groups of people. (See questions in the margin.) Paul reminds children of the first of the Ten Commandments with a promise (Exodus 20:12; Deuteronomy 5:16). **He tells children** 1) to obey parents and 2) to honor parents in the Lord. An orderly, obedient youth leads to enjoyable, peaceful old age.

**He tells fathers** 1) not to exasperate their children [taunt and tease them] and 2) to bring them up in the instruction of the Lord.

**He tells slaves, or employees** 1) to obey their earthly masters with respect, fear, and a sincere heart and 2) like slaves of Christ, to do God's will wholeheartedly—even then no one's watching (even Madam X)!

**He tells masters, or supervisors**, 1) to treat slaves (or workers) with the same respect and sincerity and 2) not to threaten them. He reminds us that God picks no favorites; He shows as much love and respect to the child as to the parent, to the slave as to the master.

List several actions you can actually do to honor

your father:

your mother:

List practical things you'll do for your children or other children in your extended family:

List your acts of kindness for your supervisor at work, at home, at school, at church:

List your acts of kindness toward your "slaves" (family members, restaurant servers, employees, medical staff, etc.):

Write one area of your life in which you'll be more obedient to God's will:

## God's Employee Handbook

*Family* and *work* are the most commonly underestimated institutions: **we need the greatest instruction for these, but receive the least**. However, the Bible provides superb instruction on how live with others at home and at work. It's God's Employee Handbook for *dulas* (slaves, or servers). Hear Him whisper: "Guard your work ethic so people won't think bad things about me or Your fellow Christians . . . even if past parental injustices haunt you—what can you do to forgive and honor your parents?"

**God's purpose is that you set a good example before your family** and your fellow employees or supervisor: that you show patience, love, and fairness before all.

Realizing that God's eye is on you all the time (and that angels and saints in heaven are cheering you on), how can you honor Him by accepting His will and purpose for your life?

So, how about it, dear Christian? Are you an obedient **person of purpose** at home and at work? Remember, you're "surrounded by . . . a great cloud of witnesses" (Hebrews 12:1), saints and angels who *cheer you on* to good behavior. (For more about these witnesses, read *Friendships of Faith*, Study 26.) Will you honor God before your family and coworkers, waiting for His reward as you walk in His will? *Extra reading*: 1 Corinthians 4:9; Hebrews 12:1–13, 22–23

## A Prayer of Purpose

*Lord, **forgive me when I lose patience with children***; *help me to love and encourage them. Guide me in showing love and respect to parents. Bless my family. **May I serve You at work**, whether I am leading others or following those in authority. Amen.*

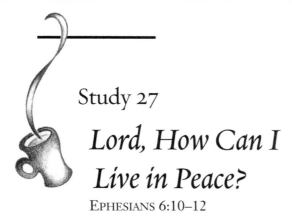

Study 27

# Lord, How Can I Live in Peace?

EPHESIANS 6:10–12

HAVE YOU EVER HAD A DAY WHEN NOTHING WENT right? Your alarm clock didn't go off on time, you had a bad hair day, a child with a terrible cough needed a trip to the doctor, your teenager refused to talk to you, your husband didn't help in the chaos . . . the list goes on and on, as Murphy's Law followed you. Remember the frustration of such a day? If that caused you stress and inner turmoil, read on.

"Marla" had not seen her husband in a year. She'd been in a Romanian prison (for convicted Christians) and hoped he was still alive in jail, too. Occasionally the officials allowed her son to visit. The women prisoners passed around any decent clothes available to the ones receiving visits, to encourage and assure their families they were all right. They spent time tending to each detail of the borrowed dresses, quickly changing, so the next woman could wear the only garment in the prison without holes. Marla was not allowed to speak to her son, but it was wonderful to see him, though he looked frail and thin.

Marla has now been released, united with her son, and has learned her husband was killed by the Communists several years ago, just before religious freedom came to Romania. As Marla tells of dressing for her son, she is following Paul's advice to put on the whole armor of God. Dressing up was her way of taking a stand against evil schemes.

My problems seem ridiculous when I compare my bad days to those of Marla. It broke my heart to read of this woman's courage, always looking up, dressing as neatly as possible, remaining very much a woman, a loving mother, a smiling encourager, always trusting Jesus that her son would survive alone, and that they would meet one day as two free Christians.

## Why Can't the World Live in Peace?

You may wonder why the world can't live in peace. You may try to make peace in your community and pray for world peace, but you must face the truth: as long as the evil one lives in the world, you won't find complete peace. What you *can* do is protect yourself from evil through God's plan of spiritual warfare.

God's purpose is not for you to give up, swamped by the latest wave of evil, shame, sickness, or fear. Triumph comes when your spirit coincides with the powerful Spirit of God, who conquers all evil (1 Corinthians 15:57). The Prince of Peace will give you perfect spiritual peace as you fight against a flawed world of conflict, confusion, and lies. "Finally, be strong in the Lord and in his mighty power. Put on the full armor of God so that you can take your stand against the devil's schemes. For your struggle is not against flesh and blood, but against the rulers, against the authorities, against the powers of this dark world and against the spiritual forces of evil in the heavenly realms" (Ephesians 6:10–12).

How do you demonstrate your strength?

In Ephesians 6:10–12, in what two things does God say we must be strong?

_____ Courage
_____ Large arm muscles
_____ The Lord
_____ A spirit of encouragement
_____ Backbone
_____ God's mighty power
_____ Faith

## Approaching Evil: Victory in Jesus

Paul advises us to be strong, not in muscular or physical power, but "in the Lord" and "in his mighty power."

In Honduras I met a missionary who worked with her husband deep in tropical jungles where witchcraft flourished. She told women in their small villages that she didn't believe in witchcraft, but they were so surrounded by these beliefs that fear kept them from becoming Christians. She finally said to them, **"My Holy Spirit is stronger** than any of your spirits." Once they got the concept of a powerful God, stronger than other powers, they gave their hearts to Him. Many left the evil practices of persecution and fear to believe in forgiveness, grace, and love that only God can give.

Sometimes **you may need the power of indirection, not direction, in hitting a bad day head-on.** How do you approach evil? Paul says, "suffering produces perseverance; perseverance, character; and character, hope" (Romans 5:3-4).

What about the evil in your world today? What imperfection is the *fly in the ointment* in your life right now? Notice one last detail: Paul says put on the *full* or *whole* armor. **Don't leave any chinks in your armor.** Leave no doubt, no holes in your faith, no hesitation or resentment in your personal relationship with the Lord. Ask God to give you perfect peace in Him, regardless of outer circumstances.

And just what is your armor? Read about these details in Study 28.

## A Prayer of Purpose

*Lord,* **thank You for giving me peace in spite of the imperfections in my stressful days.** *I'm grateful for Your loving care when I live amid conflict. Prince of Peace, give me the perfect relationship with You, to help me take a stand against evil each day. Amen.*

Study 28

# Lord, Where Is My Armor?

EPHESIANS 6:13–17

MARK TWAIN'S *A CONNECTICUT YANKEE IN KING ARTHUR'S Court* tells of the Yankee, Hank Morgan, visiting Windsor Castle in England, and seeing round holes in a suit of armor. Morgan wonders how these holes (which look like bullet holes) got into a medieval vest of armor before guns were invented. Then he is transported back to medieval times (actually knocked out at work in "a disagreement conducted with crowbars," going to England in a dream), where he himself finally shoots someone in that armor, leaving a bullet hole. I've seen those holes in the armor in Windsor Castle several times, and each time I think not only of Mark Twain but also of Ephesians 6 and God's mighty spiritual armor. Have you ever felt the fiery darts of evil? Most Christians have, but I thank God for protection against them.

As you read God's Word, find out how to use spiritual armor. Read Ephesians 6:13–17.

## The Full Armor of God

List the pieces of spiritual armor:

The belt of

The breastplate of

The boots of

The shield of

The helmet of

The sword of

## Don't Be Wishy-Washy

God asks you to put on armor for a reason: you'll be able to stand your ground when evil comes. How much evil do you see in your world today? Where are the places you need to take a stand? I know I need to stand firm in my home, church, school, the media, and other areas.

Count how many times Paul says, "Stand." First, we're *able* to stand by wearing our spiritual armor. Second, we're to stand *after* we have done everything we can. Third, we stand in a *certain way*: firm. There's no room in a Christian's purpose for wishy-washy, wet-noodle resolve! God commands: "Stand!"

The first piece of armor is **the belt of truth**. Joy Brown says in *A Special Blend*, "Have you ever wondered why in his letter to the Ephesians (6:14), Paul lists the belt of truth as the first piece of spiritual armor?" Order was important to Paul, a rabbi. Placing the *belt of truth* at the beginning of this list of armor sent a strong warning to Christians to stick to the truth. Satan's first weapon against Eve was a *distortion of the truth, or a lie*, to trick her, introducing evil into the world. Truth is a Christian's first defense against evil. Joy Brown says, "We live in a world where deception is rampant, and we have to dig deeply to find the truth. Satan seems to relish the idea of deceiving women, especially in the area of self-worth. . . . [A lie] has been so successful through the years that Satan still clings to it as his strongest weapon. Some say it's his *only* weapon."

The second piece of armor is **the breastplate of right-eousness**. As you keep the belt of truth buckled around your waist, you keep righteousness in place.

A soldier has a hard time fighting if his feet are hurting. The third piece of armor is **readiness, worn on the feet like well-fitted combat boots**. Notice readiness comes from the gospel of peace. You and I need to be ready with the gospel, to tell it to everyone (1 Peter 3:15). Christ's gospel destroys the enemy, ends war inside you, and brings peace to your heart. Your boots should be ready to carry you, with the gospel of peace on your lips, to the other side of the world—or next door.

## Jesus Is Our Total Armor

In an evil day, **strong faith is your shield**. (Review Study 14 for the measure of faith you have.) Accompanying faith is the **helmet of salvation**, a basic for protection. Make sure you know Jesus as Savior by asking Him into your heart, as a covering over you.

Are you sure you have salvation? Write what you think that includes.

*Discuss with your study friend.*

Finally, take the **sword of the Spirit, God's Word,** wherever you go. Sometimes appropriate verses from the Word will stop evil in its tracks!

Now, look back at all the pieces of armor. Do you have any holes in *your* armor? Jesus says, I am the **Truth** (John 14:6). He is the source of our **righteousness**, **peace**, **faith**, and **salvation**. He is the eternal **Word**. He is the *full armor of God*! *\*Extra reading*: John 1:1–4

## A Prayer of Purpose

*Lord, **I stand firm, on purpose, with full spiritual armor**. Enable me to be a strong force against evil where You've placed me, using truth, righteousness, and peace You've given me. Thank You for giving me faith and eternal salvation from harm, O Word. Amen.*

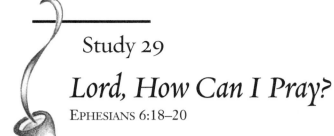

## Study 29

# *Lord, How Can I Pray?*

EPHESIANS 6:18–20

EACH STUDY IN THIS BOOK HAS CLOSED WITH A PRAYER of Purpose. Every Christian needs to learn how to pray sincere, specific, purposeful prayers. Have you ever listened to people praying who wandered around so you couldn't follow their train of thought, much less pray silently along with them? The difference in the wandering prayer and a specific one is that **prayer must have a purpose**. You may purpose to praise God in your prayers. You may thank Him for answered prayer. You may decide to pray for personal purity for yourself, or to intercede fervently for someone else. You may listen prayerfully, asking God to commune with you. When evil surrounds you, you pray intently for rescue.

Coming home from a Christian conference in San Jose, California, my car ran hot. Unfortunately, I was five hours from home, so I had to spend two days in a hotel while an auto shop crew repaired it. Seven hundred dollars later, I left San Jose; and as I drove by Rockville, my car stopped. Of course, I prayed. Well, to tell the truth, I whined. (Sometimes I do a lot of whining as I commune with God!) Seeing an exit just ahead, I walked in high heels to a filling station, sliding on the gravel down the exit ramp and tearing my hose. I asked a tattoo-covered, red-haired (with black roots) lady . . . uh, woman . . . in a glass cage to let me use the phone. She waved me to a pay phone, where I called my road service. (My cellular phone, of course, wouldn't work.)

When the road service came, the man flirted with the lady in the cage, ignoring me. Feeling isolated and recognizing evil all around me, I called my office to let my secretary know where I was. Then I interrupted the road service man propositioning the woman in the cage to ask for a gas can, thinking I may have been out of gas, but the woman in the cage used foul language, refused to help me with gas, and told me I was irresponsible to break down there. I had trouble keeping a Christian spirit, tempted to lash out at her or sit down and cry. Have you ever had a day like that? The only thing you can do is pray.

## God Answers Before We Ask

Miraculously, **God was answering my prayer before I even began**. My coworker on the road called into our office, my secretary overhead the conversation, asked *his* secretary where he was, and she responded, "Five miles from Rockville." My secretary called back on the pay phone to let me know he'd pick me up in five minutes.

God also answered the prayer of a teenager in back, who lent me a gas can. He asked if I were a Christian.

"Yes," I said.

"I thought so." He'd been praying for a Christian example and he noticed the way I reacted in the face of profanity and other adversity. As God answered my prayer, my coworker took me home, the repair shop paid for the towing, and all was well. Looking back, I wonder why I didn't pray with purpose for the teenager; somehow I hardly noticed him with the dynamics of my torn hose, the stalled car, the mean woman in the cage, and the Casanova road service man. I should have been alert to pray, as Paul says, "And pray in the Spirit on all occasions with all kinds of prayers and requests. With this in mind, be alert and always keep on praying for all the saints. Pray also for me, that whenever I open my mouth, words may be given me so that I will fearlessly make known the mystery of the gospel, for which I am an ambassador in chains. Pray that I may declare it fearlessly, as I should" (Ephesians 6:18–20).

Read verses 18–20. Then answer these questions:

What kinds of prayers have you lifted up to God this week?

Name them, if any:

How long has it been since you've prayed for the saints (Christians you know)?

What does it mean to pray for an "ambassador in chains"?

Unlike Edna at the gas station, how can you open your mouth and declare the gospel fearlessly?

Share your answers with your study friend.

## Keep on Praying for all the Saints

Instead of surface prayers, God gives three ways to pray:

**1. Pray in the Spirit**, that is, directed by the Holy Spirit as you pray, open to pray as He nudges.

**2.** He also asks you to **be alert**, not tiring as you pray for other Christians.

**3.** Finally, he asks you to **pray for fearlessness** among Christians, as they share the mystery of the gospel.

With these three purposes in mind, pray with praise, confession, requests, and intercession.

## A Prayer of Purpose

*Lord, forgive me for not praying according to Your purpose.* **Help me not to be so absorbed in my minor circumstances that I fail to give a fearless witness.** *I pray now for those in chains suffering for Christ. Fill them with peace and joy in Your purpose. Amen.*

# Study 30

# O God, Give Me Your Grace

EPHESIANS 6:21–24

THOMAS ELLISON, MY BROTHER-IN-LAW, VISITED ME TODAY IN my new home. My husband, his brother, died twenty-five years ago, but Thomas is still in the family. We talked about good times from the past. A faithful Christian, Thomas told me the story of "Brad," who'd once tried to commit suicide, but because of my husband's tender words during the crisis, Brad changed his mind. God had given grace to my husband as he spoke words of hope. Brad received that grace, decided to ask Jesus into his heart, and began a life of purpose. Recently he'd shared his story with Thomas, who didn't know the connection between his own brother and Brad. Thomas then shared that precious grace with me, carrying the message of the hope my husband had shared with Brad years ago. I was grateful for Thomas and this poignant story; I told him we'd always be family. More than being in-law kin in the Ellison clan, we've a higher relationship: brother and sister in the family of God! **We have a friendship of purpose, centered in God's will.**

Paul knew the hope that comes from being joined with Christian friends by the grace of God. He even accepted his position in prison by the will of God, obedient to the end. Like Thomas, carrying a message to me, Tychicus, Paul's brother in Christ, carried a message of grace and hope to the Ephesians. Paul knew they were "forever friends," with a special bond: their friendship went all the way to heaven. He says, "Tychicus, the dear brother and faithful servant in the Lord, will tell you everything, so that you also may know how I am and what I am doing. I am sending him to you for this very purpose, that you may know how we are, and that he may encourage you. Peace to the brothers, and love with faith from God the Father and the Lord Jesus Christ. Grace to all who love our Lord Jesus Christ with an undying love" (Ephesians 6:21–24).

How is Tychicus identified?

1. _____

2. _____

*Friend to Friend*

## Friend to Friend

How can you serve as a *dear sister* and *faithful servant* to your friends?

What is the purpose of Tychicus' visit?

1. That the Ephesians may know _____.

2. That Tychicus may _____ the Ephesians.

### Forever Friends

Tychicus, Paul's letter carrier, is identified as a dear brother and faithful servant. The word translated *dear* means *cherished*, or *of worth, worthy*. **As a cherished sister to your girlfriends, how can you become a faithful servant to them?** You can encourage them, make them feel worthy, and give good Christian advice. If you draw them nearer to Christ, *your friendship becomes one of purpose and worth*. You become a woman worthy of servanthood. *Extra reading about Tychicus*: Colossians 4:7–9.

Paul wrote his forever friends in Ephesus to let them know how he was, what he was doing—but more importantly, to *encourage* the young Ephesian Christians. You can encourage others, making them your forever friends. My grandmother used to say about our family: "Blood is thicker than water." Jesus' blood can bring your friends into the family of God. **Your purpose, like Paul's, can be to bring friends into the family**.

### Love Him with an Undying Love

A desperate woman with no family jumped from a bridge to commit suicide. A stranger jumped into the water to save her. As she pushed him away, he began to flounder, and she realized he was drowning. Even in her despair, she couldn't let him

List things you can do with acquaintances to make them "forever friends."

Share with your study friend at least one thing you'll do as follow-up to this study.

drown. She dragged him to shore, later saying, "I wasn't saved by a *person*, but by a *purpose*." She became a woman of purpose: repaying him for giving her purpose in life. His family asked her to join them as family, and she became a Christian and a close family friend.

Write your purpose in life in one sentence.

What other aims fall under your purpose?

Now write a vision statement of that purpose:

**Believing in Jesus as my Savior, I, _____ (your name) will be a woman of purpose by:**
[write several objectives for your life, under which you can decide later on actions that follow your overall purpose]

Share this vision statement with your study friend.

According to verses 21–24, what accompanies peace and love? Paul says it's faith. We all have the same measure of fullness, or faith (Study 14). Now's the time to exercise yours. Has God been nudging you to step out in faith, *following a purpose He's given you* in life? **Today, act on that purpose.** *Extra reading*: Matthew 17:20–21

In this last study, review previous studies in which God has spoken to you. As you pray the last Prayer of Purpose in this book, ask Him what *He* wants to do *through you*. I pray your life will be changed by prayerful study of His Word, and you'll act on your understanding. Paul reminds you in the last sentence of Ephesians, "love our Lord Jesus Christ with an undying love." **Don't yawn in the face of God and go back to sleep.**

## A Prayer of Purpose

*Lord, I love You with an undying love. I praise You for loving me and giving me abundant grace. Thank You for dying for me. I want to be, like Tychicus, a sibling in Christ, Your sister and faithful servant.* **I will be a woman of purpose for You.** *Amen.*

# Friend to Friend Notes

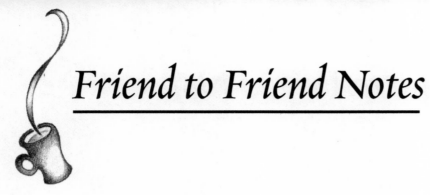

# Friend to Friend Notes

# Friend to Friend Notes

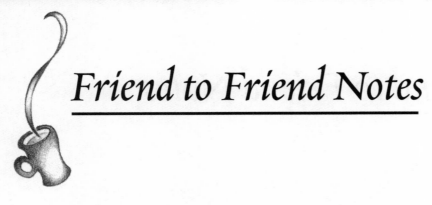

# Friend to Friend Notes

# Also by Edna Ellison
# in the Friend to Friend series

Friendships of Faith:
A Shared Study of Hebrews

N034120 • 1-56309-762-1

Friend to Friend:
Enriching Friendships Through
a Shared Study of Philippians

N024118 • 1-56309-710-9

# Available in Christian bookstores everywhere.

new
hope
PUBLISHERS

*Inspiring Women. Changing Lives.*